John Woolman

A Nonviolence and Social Change Source Book

John Woolman

A Nonviolence and Social Change Source Book

2nd Edition

Edited by
Sterling P. Olmsted and Mike Heller

Wilmington College Peace Resource Center
Wilmington, Ohio
&
Friends United Press
Richmond, Indiana

Edited by Sterling P. Olmsted and Mike Heller

The Friends United Press has generously given permission to reprint passages from Phillips P. Moulton's edition of *The Journal and Major Essays of John Woolman* (Richmond, IN: Friends United Press, 1989).

With appreciation to the following libraries for permission to use photographs of these documents: For the cover photograph of *Woolman's Journal, Manuscript B*, first page, and pages from *The Works of John Woolman, 1774*, thanks to the Friends Historical Library at Swarthmore College; for *A First Book for Children*, thanks to the Library of the Society of Friends (LSF), Friends House, London; and for John Woolman's letter to his wife Sarah, 31st, 7th month, 1772, Woolman Papers, thanks to the Historical Society of Pennsylvania (HSP).

Design by Mary Ann Mayers, www.ExtraordinaryLives.com

Published by:
Wilmington College Peace Resource Center, 1870 Quaker Way,
Pyle Center Box 1183, Wilmington, OH 45177
&
Friends United Press, 101 Quaker Hill Dr., Richmond, IN 47374

ISBN-13: 978-0-9658866-5-9

Contents

Illustrations

Preface to the Second Edition

This second edition of *John Woolman: A Nonviolence and Social Change Source Book* is updated and improved throughout. Unlike other books on John Woolman, this book brings together, in one volume, major passages from Woolman's *Journal*, selections from his letters, a sampling of his essays and other writings, observations about Woolman by his contemporaries, background information, items not previously published, and a study guide with discussion questions. The book is intended to be useful for courses, discussion groups, and individuals.

John Woolman stands out among colonial American writers not only because of the unusual expression of his faith, which made his *Journal* a classic among spiritual autobiographies, but also because of his far-reaching ideas about peace, equality, and simplicity, which are still influencing people. Unlike perhaps any other colonial American writer, Woolman's ways of working for nonviolence and for effective interactions with others continue to be a source of inspiration and ideas for us today. Hence this book, which we hope will broaden that influence.

Readers have often noted how Woolman's writings express a spirit of tenderness at the same time that they are powerfully persuasive. He spoke for the universality of God's love and a tender feeling for all humanity. He had a vision of the equality of all human beings that inspired his life-long work against slavery. He saw that keeping slaves was not only horribly oppressive for those in slavery but also oppressive and dangerous for the owners and their children who would inherit slaves. He sought to show the owners how liberating their slaves would free themselves and their children from this oppression. Similarly, he sought to help both poor laborers as well as their wealthy landowners. He was far ahead of his time in his interest in not only helping but also learning from American Indians, although his efforts with the Indians were more limited.

Sterling Olmsted and I began to compile this book in the mid-1990s and the first edition was published in 1997. Sterling, who passed away in November 2011 at age 96, was a beloved teacher and friend. He and his wife Barbara Starr Olmsted, who died in 2004, were widely appreciated, loved, and respected. They made many contributions to the Religious Society of

Friends, Friends' organizations, and the community of Wilmington College in Wilmington, Ohio. Barbara was very important to our completing the first edition of this book. They both were great friends to me.

He continued his scholarly work well into his nineties when he was putting together a book on Lucretia Mott. Before Sterling died he saw the publication in 2011 of the second book in this series, *Mohandas K. Gandhi: The Last Eighteen Years*. All of these were labors of love.

Sterling understood John Woolman's contributions to humanity perhaps better than anyone. He often spoke of Woolman's advice, in "A Plea for the Poor," to consider "the connection of things," and applied Woolman's ideas for peace and justice to world events today.

Acknowledgements

My thanks to Ruth Olmsted, Sterling and Barbara's daughter, who supported this work throughout and who joined me to complete the Gandhi book in this series. My thanks to Neil Snarr for his many labors to see this book through publication, and to Jon Kershner for his valuable help. For caring support for this publication, thanks go to James Boland and the staff of the Peace Resource Center, Wilmington College, and Annie Glen and the staff of Friends United Press. Thanks to the staff of the Library of the Society of Friends, Friends House, London, for assistance with corrections to "Concerning the Ministry," based upon a recently located manuscript. I greatly appreciate Mary Ann Mayers of Extraordinary Lives for her excellent editing and book design. I could not have completed this work without the loving support of Rebecca Heller.

Mike Heller

The Nonviolence and Social Change Source Book Series

The concept for this series grew from a Wilmington College Peace Studies course entitled "Woolman and Gandhi." In that course, students studied John Woolman and Mohandas K. Gandhi, and wrote seminar papers on other agents of social change. Later, the course title was changed to "Nonviolence and Social Change," Thich Nhat Hanh was added to the general reading, and seminar topics were expanded.

The *Source Book* series was designed with this and other Peace Studies courses in mind. However, the series may prove useful in study groups and in a wider range of college courses including Autobiography, American Studies, Women's Studies, Comparative Religion, and Non-Western Studies. *The John Woolman Source Book* may be used independently or as a supplement to Phillips P. Moulton's edition of *The Journal and Major Essays of John Woolman.*

This new edition of the *John Woolman Source Book* updates the series; a *Gandhi Source Book* is already in publication. Books on Lucretia Mott, Dorothy Day, Jeanette Rankin, Abdul Gaffer Khan, and Bayard Rustin are in the planning stages. The list may eventually be much longer.

Each book consists of selected writings of the change agent, with added background material and notes to make the writings more understandable to readers. Each also includes discussion topics and questions.

From our perspective, we are all social change agents whether we intend to be or not. What we say, what we write, how we spend our time and our money, how we relate to other people and to the world around us—they all have an effect on how the human family lives now and in the future.

If we wish to become more intentional in our actions, it is useful to know what these extraordinary people did, what belief structures sustained them, and what they needed in the way of knowledge, skill, community support, and social tradition.

Some of the general questions posed in these source books are designed not only to enable readers to compare one change agent with another, but also to gain some sense of what it means to be an intentional agent of social change:

1. What issues and problems did these persons choose to deal with? Which of these issues and problems are still with us?
2. How did these persons see these problems and issues? How did they arrive at their particular perspectives?
3. What methods did they use? Are their methods applicable today?
4. How much importance did they place on attending to spiritual process rather than seeking results?

Sterling Olmsted
Mike Heller

Introduction:
Background for the Study of John Woolman

John Woolman, an American Quaker, was a travelling minister in the Philadelphia Yearly Meeting of the Religious Society of Friends. Born in 1720, he would be the eldest son of thirteen children. His grandfather had settled in West Jersey in the late 17th century, and Woolman lived in Mt. Holly, New Jersey in the midst of a network of relatives and other Friends. He belonged to the Burlington (N.J.) Meeting of Friends, as did his wife, Sarah Ellis, whom he married in 1749 at age twenty-nine. They had two children, a son who died in infancy and a daughter Mary, who married John Comfort and was the mother of ten children.

After being recorded as a minister in 1742, Woolman traveled widely among Friends. Like many of his American contemporaries, he owned land and provided for most of his family's needs by farming. He earned money by selling fruit from his farm and a variety of other endeavors—by keeping a store for a time, and by tailoring, land surveying, writing legal papers, and teaching in a one-room school. His travels in the ministry, which began when he was twenty-three and continued for nearly thirty years, were not a means of making a living. Members of the Society of Friends who travelled in the ministry did not expect payment for their services, although lodging and other assistance were supplied by the Friends they visited. To ease additional financial burden and to support one another, Friends in their home meeting probably assumed some responsibility for their families while they were away.

Many of his trips were of short duration, but before his marriage he made a three-month journey through the Southern colonies in 1745, and a four-month journey to New England in 1746. After his marriage, he stayed close to home until 1757 when he revisited the Southern colonies. Three years later he made a second visit to New England. Most noteworthy, perhaps because he recounted them in some detail, were his journey to the Indians at Wyalusing in 1763 and his final journey in 1772 to England, where he died of smallpox while in York.

He was active in the affairs of Philadelphia Yearly Meeting (to which Burlington belonged), serving on various committees including the Overseers of the Press, and taking part in the drafting of Epistles on issues of general concern. During his lifetime, he published two essays "On the Keeping of Negroes," the first in 1754, the second in 1762, as well as a collection of shorter essays. *The Journal* and "A Plea for the Poor" were published after his death.

As a social change agent, Woolman is best known for his efforts to persuade members of the Society of Friends that the institution of slavery was contrary to their belief in the sacredness and equality of individuals. While it is not possible to quantify Woolman's actual influence, and there were other members active in the same cause, the most notable of which was Anthony Benezet, there is little doubt that he had significant influence on beliefs and actions relating to slavery. By 1774, two years after Woolman's death, the Philadelphia Yearly Meeting had made disownment the penalty for selling or transferring slaves, and two years later local meetings were directed to "testify their disunion" with any Friend who did not free his or her slaves. Similar actions were taking place in other Yearly Meetings as well. Thus, in the 1770s, Friends became the first large group in America to take a stand against slavery and to emancipate their slaves.

Woolman also influenced other social issues through his actions and writings. During the French and Indian War, Woolman resisted the payment of war taxes. His opposition to slavery expanded to include other forms of oppression. He became acutely aware of growing inequities around him as the rich became visibly richer, and he argued against the production of "superfluities." He understood, however, that forgoing luxuries might result in increased unemployment, and so suggested that more people could be employed in the production of necessities, a solution known as "feather bedding" in later times. He argued that the rich should require fewer luxuries for themselves, reduce rents charged to the poor, and hire more people to reduce oppressive working conditions and poverty. On his visit to England, he was distressed at the plight of workers in the mills, exclaiming in his *Journal*, "May those who have plenty lay these things to heart!"

He was also greatly concerned about the plight of Native Americans and the conflict between them and the settlers on the frontier. He was aware of the impairment of the environment through over-tilling of the land, over-cutting of the forest, and over-hunting and fishing. He was concerned about children and young people, specifically the inadequacy of their schooling. He taught school in Mt. Holly for several years, wrote an essay "On Schools," and published a primer that seems designed to implement his ideas on pedagogy.

The Religious Society of Friends (Quakers)

In order to understand John Woolman it is important to know something about the faith community in which he was active.

The Quaker movement, which became the Religious Society of Friends, began in Britain during the religious ferments and upheavals of the seventeenth century. Early adherents saw their movement as "Primitive Christianity Revived." Many of their contemporaries saw it as a radical challenge to established religion. The leader of the movement, George Fox, although deeply immersed in the Bible, emphasized the continuing work of the Spirit and the possibility of receiving fresh instruction from the Teacher within. The movement rejected the authority of the established church and the need for outward sacraments.

Fox and other leaders travelled about the British Isles, the North American continent, the Caribbean, and parts of Europe, speaking often before large groups. Friends gathered openly for worship, even when such meetings were unlawful. They refused to take oaths in court. They used the singular forms "thee" and "thou" with people of higher social status who expected them to use the plural "you." They refused to take off their hats to anyone. It is not surprising that they were viewed with alarm and thrown into prison or severely punished in other ways.

Though most adherents in the beginning were of humble origin, the movement soon attracted some with influence and power. One of these was William Penn, the son of Admiral Penn. He sought and obtained a grant of land in America, and encouraged fellow Quakers to settle there. As proprietor of Pennsylvania, William Penn endeavored to treat the Indians fairly, and helped establish freedom of conscience, a policy that brought to the colony many people of various religious persuasions who were suffering persecution in Europe.

Though the colony founded as a "holy experiment" did not live up to all of Penn's dreams, Pennsylvania remained for several decades under Quaker control. With West Jersey, which had been settled a decade earlier by Quakers, it became a major center of Quaker activity in North America. There were also important Quaker settlements from Massachusetts to North Carolina.

As the Quaker movement developed into the Religious Society of Friends in Britain and North America, it gradually became an organization with its own distinctive procedures, its own version of Christian faith and practice. The local worshipping congregation, called a "meeting" rather than a "church," was the primary organization. Gathering at least once a week for worship, and managing its own affairs through a monthly meeting for business, it was called a Monthly Meeting. Monthly Meetings in the same geographical area constituted a Quarterly Meeting, which met every three months; Quarterly Meetings were joined together in a Yearly Meeting. Thus, a time-space structure replaced the more hierarchical structure of most religious bodies. Philadelphia Yearly Meeting, to which Woolman belonged, included meetings in New Jersey as well as Pennsylvania.

Friends met for worship in plain meetinghouses, without altar or pulpit. There was no paid minister, no stated order of worship. People settled into silence and spoke out of the silence. Those who appeared to have special gifts in ministry were recognized as ministers by the Monthly Meeting and usually sat on the facing benches, but any man or woman might speak as he or she felt led. Men sat on one side of the meetinghouse during worship, women on the other, and men and women met separately for business. But both men and women who had been recognized by the meeting (recorded as ministers) travelled in the ministry with the approval of the meeting. This travelling ministry, in which John Woolman participated, served as a means of stimulating and uniting a scattered people.

In meetings for business Friends sought to maintain a worshipful spirit and to follow God's leadings in making decisions. A clerk presided. There were no formal motions as in parliamentary procedure, no votes; decisions were made by finding unity. On any matter being discussed, it was the task of the clerk to try to gather the "sense of the meeting." Friends with contrary views expressed their disagreements. An individual who could not support a decision might "stand aside" and allow the action to go forward. Progress was sometimes slow, but actions would be strongly supported when unity was achieved.

Members joining the meeting were not required to subscribe to a stated set of beliefs. There were, however, principles of conduct and action on which Friends had united, called testimonies.

Most fully spelled out was the peace testimony, in which English Friends in the seventeenth century declared to Charles II that they "utterly deny… all outward wars and strife and fightings with outward weapons, for any end or under any pretense whatsoever" (Fox 399). This testimony created problems for Friends in North America, which was at times a battleground for the European powers. Adhering to the peace testimony was particularly difficult while Friends were serving in the government of Pennsylvania, and this led prominent Friends to give up their positions in the Assembly during the French and Indian War. During the American Revolution, many Friends suffered severe penalties when they refused to support either the colonists or the English. Friends who let themselves be drawn into the conflict were disciplined by their meetings, and some were eventually disowned.

Friends already shared a testimony of equality (women and men, people of high and low social status), and through the efforts of Woolman and others, they were expanding the equality testimony to include opposition to slavery. They also had a testimony of simplicity that advised Friends to avoid excessive materialism and "superfluities," and to seek a certain "plainness" in their speech, dress, and furniture. Woolman and other Friends sought to establish a renewed adherence to both the equality and simplicity testimonies.

Woolman's World

John Woolman's farm, his tailor shop, and his meeting were in New Jersey just across the Delaware River from Philadelphia. Noah Webster, writing in *American Selection* (1794), a school textbook published two decades after Woolman's death, describes Philadelphia as:

...the largest and most regular city in America. Its streets cross each other at right angles and form the whole city into squares. Near the center is Market street, which is wider than the others, and contains the largest and best supplied market in America, or perhaps in the world. The Statehouse is a magnificent structure, and the garden belonging to it has been lately improved and laid out in agreeable walks for the recreation of the citizens.

The hospital, the poor house, and prison, the two former of brick, and the latter of stone, are noble buildings and exceed any of the kind in this country. The new German reformed church is the most magnificent of the kind in America, and was built at the expense of ten thousand pounds. This city contains more than five thousand houses, and fifty thousand inhabitants. It is at the head of navigation, about one hundred and fifty miles from the mouth of the Delaware. (103)

The Philadelphia that Woolman knew was smaller and not as impressive as that described by Webster, but was already a major urban center.

In the English colonies as a whole, population grew during Woolman's lifetime from just under half a million in 1720 to over two million in 1770; in New Jersey and Pennsylvania the population grew from about 60,000 to nearly 360,000 in the same period (Bureau of the Census 1168). Growth was fueled by both large families and continuing immigration (by 1790, one third of the population of Pennsylvania was of German origin).

Commerce was becoming the way to wealth, and the overseas demand for wheat, rice and other commodities was inducing farmers to spend less effort in supplying their families and more in producing for foreign trade. Rich farmers and merchants were getting richer, living in greater luxury, and demanding more manufactured items from overseas. This was in accord with the expectations of the mother country, which regarded the colonies primarily as a source of commodities and raw materials, and a market for manufactured goods.

The factory system was getting under way in England, although the only available forms of energy were human, animal, wind and water-power. Weaving and spinning mills were established in Birmingham and Northampton in 1742, but the first steam engine was not installed in a spinning mill until 1785. On his visit to England in 1772, Woolman saw something of what his younger contemporary William Blake would call the "dark satanic mills." Woolman was appalled at the exploitation of workers.

The use of slave labor, which had begun in 1619 in Virginia, was still growing in the colonies, although opposition to slavery was also growing. The number of Africans, mostly slaves, grew from 69,000 in 1720 to 460,000 in 1770. Most of this growth was in the Southern colonies, but even in New Jersey and Pennsylvania the number increased from 2,400 to 14,000. In 1746, thirty percent of laborers in Philadelphia were slaves, and it is estimated that in 1762, five hundred slaves were imported for sale in Philadelphia ("British Settlements" 182), the same years that Woolman was writing his first and second essays on slavery.

Penn's initial efforts to deal fairly with the Native Americans eroded as new waves of European settlers moved to the frontier in search of unoccupied farmland. Bloody conflicts ensued, becoming intense during the French and Indian War (1755–1762). Woolman's visit to the Indians at Wyalusing in 1763 was related to his concern for what was happening on the frontier.

There was no system of universal public education in Pennsylvania and New Jersey, although schools of various kinds and at various levels were being established. Woolman himself ran a school in Mt. Holly, and his contemporary and close friend Anthony Benezet taught for forty years at Germantown and Philadelphia. Benezet also established a school for girls, and ran an evening school in his home for children of slaves.

Average life span was short, infant mortality high. One of the great scourges was smallpox. Inoculation against smallpox was introduced in England in 1717, but was widely regarded as hazardous, and was in fact much more so than the later practice of vaccination. Jonathan Edwards, having just been appointed President of Nassau Hall (Princeton), not far from Mt. Holly, died in 1758 from aftereffects of being inoculated. Benjamin Franklin was an early opponent of inoculation, but changed his mind. Woolman refused inoculation, and died of smallpox in England. Years later, in 1797, his daughter died of smallpox (Amelia Mott Gummere, ed., *The Journal and Essays of John Woolman*, 42).

Intellectually, Woolman's world was in ferment. Religious revival charged with emotion on the one hand, and increasing dependence on reason and common sense on the other, pulled in different directions. Jonathan Edwards' uncharacteristically dark sermon, "Sinners in the Hands of an Angry God" in 1741, and the earlier preaching of John Wesley and George Whitefield, moved many during the "The Great Awakening." In the following decades, Franklin and Jefferson, drawing on John Locke, David Hume, and French intellectuals in what has been called "The Enlightenment," emphasized natural rights and the possibility of a rational and humane society with freedom and greater equality for all.

Woolman may well have been affected by both streams. He was concerned for the spiritual condition of the people he met, but Locke's *On Education* was in his personal library. His ideas often seem consonant with those of the Enlightenment, tempered by his Quakerism and his loving concern for all human beings.

1. New Jersey, Pennsylvania and the Journey to Wyalusing

On the map below, Mt. Holly, NJ, is Woolman's home, and Burlington is the location of his Quaker Monthly Meeting. Philadelphia, across the Delaware River, is the seat of the Philadelphia Yearly Meeting that included New Jersey and Delaware along with eastern Pennsylvania. Ft. Allen and Wyalusing are points on Woolman's 200-mile journey to visit the Indians. Other place names will help to orient the reader.

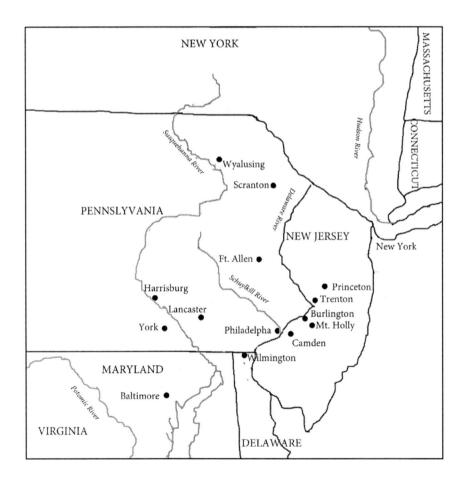

2. The Journey to Long Island and New England

The New England journey, as reported in chapter 7 of *The Journal*, was one of Woolman's longer trips. All the places on the map are mentioned within the chapter or by Mercy Redman in her journal. (She refers to the city of New York as York.) It is difficult to trace Woolman's exact route, as he took side trips to Boston and to Nantucket.

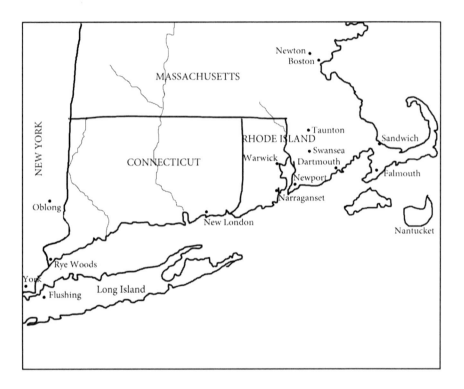

3. Woolman in England

Woolman's journey through England in 1772 is narrated in chapter 12 of *The Journal*. He travelled on foot from London to York, going by a somewhat indirect route to Lancaster and Kendal in northwest England. Places in bold-face type are among those mentioned in *The Journal* or in other records. Other places are included to provide orientation for the present-day reader.

SCOTLAND

• **Kendal**

• **Lancaster**

• **York**

Manchester
•

• **Huddlesfield**

•Liverpool

•**Sheffield**

Nottingham •

Birmingham
•

• **Coventry**

• **Warwick**

• Cambridge

ENGLAND

WALES

•Oxford

• **Hertford**

London •

• Bristol

Canterbury •

Plymouth
•

Woolman Chronology and Context of Events

1701 Yale founded

1703 John Wesley 1703-91

1704 Jonathan Edwards 1704-58

1705 John Churchman 1705-75

1706 Benjamin Franklin 1706-90

1710 Population of Colonial America 327,360

1711 David Hume 1711-76

1712 Jean J. Rousseau 1712-78

1713 Anthony Benezet 1713-84

1715 Israel Pemberton 1715-70

1718 William Penn dies

1720 John Woolman born 10/19 in Rancocas, NJ; Population 467,465

1723 Adam Smith 1723-90

1724 Immanuel Kant 1724-1804

1727 George II becomes King

1729 Baltimore founded

1730 Methodism founded; Population 636,045

1732   George Washington 1732-99; *Poor Richard's Almanac*

1734   Slave revolt in NJ

1735   John Adams 1735-1826; Peter Zenger acquitted

1736   Woolman experiences spiritual conflicts; Jonathan Edwards' *A Faithful Narrative*

1737   "Walking Purchase"; Thomas Paine 1737-1807

1739   Moravian Church in America founded

1740   Population 912,742

1741   Woolman moves to Mt. Holly

1742   Woolman begins speaking in Meeting

1743   Woolman travels in NJ (2 weeks); Thomas Jefferson 1743-1826

1746   Woolman works as a tailor; Southern journey; Princeton University founded

1747   Woolman travels to Long Island and NE; Hume's *Concerning Human Understanding*

1748   Woolman travels to NJ and MD; Elias Hicks 1748-1830

1749   Woolman marries Sarah Ellis; Henry Fielding's *Tom Jones*

1750   Woolman's father dies and his daughter Mary born; Population 1,186,408

1751   Woolman travels in NJ

1753 Woolman travels in PA; Refuses to write will

1754 Woolman's son is born and dies; "On Negroes, Part I"; King's College founded

1755 "Pacifist Epistle"; "War-Tax Epistle"; Braddock defeated

1756 Woolman gives up merchandising; Begins writing *The Journal*; Quakers quit PA Assembly

1757 Woolman travels in MD, VA, and NC

1758 "On Trade"; Woolman quarters soldiers; Philadelphia Yearly Meeting (PYM) adopts a formal minute urging Friends to free slaves; Fall of Quebec; Smallpox epidemic

1759 Woolman begins teaching; Refuses inoculation

1760 Woolman travels in NE; George III becomes King; Population 1,593,625

1761 Woolman gives up dyed clothing

1762 "On Negroes, Part II"; Rousseau's *Social Contract*

1763 Woolman visits Indians; "A Plea for the Poor"; French and Indian War ends

1764 Woolman visits NJ coast; Brown University founded

1765 Stamp Act passed

1766 Woolman travels on foot in DE, NJ; Stamp Act repealed; Right to tax affirmed

1767   Woolman travels on foot in MD, NJ

1768   "On True Wisdom"; Woolman travels on foot in MD; Boston refuses to quarter troops

1769   Woolman considers trip to West Indies

1770   Woolman has attack of pleurisy; "On True Harmony"; New England Yearly Meeting (NEYM) requires emancipation of slaves; Boston "Massacre"

1771   Mary Woolman marries John Comfort; Population 2,165,076

1772   Woolman travels to England; Dies in York, England; Committees of Correspondence

1773   Boston Tea Party

1774   Woolman's works published; PYM makes slaveholding a disownable offense; Lexington and Concord

1776   Declaration of Independence; Smith's *Wealth of Nations*

1777   Battle of Saratoga

1778   Congress prohibits importation of slaves

1780   PYM disowns slave sellers; Population 2,797,854

1781   North Carolina Yearly Meeting expels Friends who don't free slaves

1782   NEYM reports all clear of slave-holding

1783   Peace of Paris signed

1784 Kant's *Critique of Pure Reason*

1786 Shays' Rebellion 1787; NYYM reports all clear of slave-holding

1788 Constitution postpones anti-slavery action for 20 years

1789 Washington inaugurated

1790 Franklin dies; Adam Smith dies; Population 3,929,625

1791 Bill of Rights added to Constitution

1793 "Plea for the Poor" published; French Reign of Terror; Lucretia Mott 1793-1880

1794 Paine's *Age of Reason*

1795 Napoleon Commander in Chief in France

1797 Adams inaugurated

1798 Malthus's *On Population*

1799 Washington dies

1800 Population 5,308,483

Selections from
The Journal

A

JOURNAL

OF THE

LIFE, GOSPEL LABOURS,

AND

CHRISTIAN EXPERIENCES

OF THAT

FAITHFUL MINISTER

OF

JESUS CHRIST,

JOHN WOOLMAN,

Late of MOUNT-HOLLY, in the Province of
NEW-JERSEY.

ISAIAH xxxii. 17.

*The work of righteousness shall be peace ; and the effect of righteous-
ness, quietness and assurance for ever.*

PHILADELPHIA:

Printed by JOSEPH CRUKSHANK, in Market-Street, between
Second and Third Streets.

M.DCC.LXXIV.

Title page of The Works of John Woolman,
published by Joseph Crukshank, 1774

A
J O U R N A L

OF THE

LIFE AND TRAVELS

OF

JOHN WOOLMAN,

IN THE SERVICE OF THE GOSPEL.

C H A P. I.

*His birth and parentage, with some account of
the operations of divine grace on his mind in
his youth — His first appearance in the ministry — And his considerations, while young,
on the keeping of slaves.*

I HAVE often felt a motion of love
to leave some hints in writing of my experience of the goodness of God: and
now, in the thirty-sixth year of my age, I
begin this work.

I was born in Northampton, in Burlington county, West-Jersey, in the Year 1720;
and before I was seven years old I began to

B   be

First page of The Journal, *in* The Works of John Woolman, *1774*

I have fometimes felt a neceffity to ftand up, but that fpirit which is of the world hath fo much prevailed in many, and the pure life of truth been fo preffed down, that I have gone forward, not as one travelling in a road caft up, and well prepared, but as a man walking through a miry place, in which are ftones here and there, fafe to ftep on ; but fo fituated that one ftep being taken, time is neceffary to fee where to ftep next.

Now I find that in the pure obedience, the mind learns contentment, in appearing weak and foolifh to that wifdom which is of the world ; and in thefe lowly labours, they who ftand in a low place, rightly exercifed under the crofs, will find nourifhment.

The gift is pure, and while the eye is fingle in attending thereto, the underftanding is preferved clear ; felf is kept out ; we rejoice in filling up that which remains of the afflictions of Chrift, for his body's fake, which is the church.

The natural man loveth eloquence, and many love to hear eloquent orations ; and if there is not a careful attention to the gift, men who have once labour'd in the pure gofpel miniftry, growing weary of fuffering, and afhamed of appearing weak, may kindle a fire, compafs themfelves about with fparks, and walk in the light ; not of Chrift who is under fuffering ; but of that fire, which they, going from the gift, have kindled : And that in hearers, which is gone from the meek fuffering ftate, into the worldly wifdom, may

be

Third page of "Concerning the Ministry," in
The Works of John Woolman, *1774*

Quaker journals are neither private diaries nor autobiographies; rather, they are personal accounts of the writers' experiences with God, or the leadings of God within. They were written for others to read but were seldom published until after the writers' deaths. They were sometimes printed by a meeting or a committee so that others, who were trying to discern and understand their own leadings, could have a record of someone else's experiences. Before sailing for England in 1772, John Woolman left the first ten chapters of The Journal *with the Overseers of the Press of the Philadelphia Yearly Meeting. Chapters 11 and 12 were written on shipboard or in England.*

The first three chapters were written when Woolman was thirty-five. They are, therefore, the work of a middle-aged man looking back on his early life. Most of the other chapters were written closer to the described events. The account in chapter 8 of the 1763 journey to the Indians has many dated entries, as do chapters 9 and 12. Other chapters are at times summaries, at times detailed accounts.

Selections from The Journal *are from the text edited by Phillips Moulton, published originally by Oxford University Press and reprinted by Friends United Press. The* Journal *has been published many times, but the Moulton edition has become the authoritative text. The text of* The Journal *and the editor's footnotes are presented here as in the Moulton edition, without grammatical or usage corrections.*

Chapter 1
1720–1742

I have often felt a motion of love to leave some hints in writing of my experience of the goodness of God, and now, in the thirty-sixth year of my age, I begin this work.[1] I was born in Northampton, in Burlington County in West Jersey, A.D. 1720, and before I was seven years old I began to be acquainted with the operations of divine love. Through the care of my parents, I was taught to read near as soon as I was capable of it, and as I went from school one Seventh Day, I remember, while my companions went to play by the

---

1.   In Manuscript C, the earliest surviving version of *The Journal*, the first sentence reads, "I have often felt a desire to leave some brief hints in writing concerning my experience of the Goodness of God." Amelia Mott Gummere, ed.,*The Journal and Essays of John Woolman,* (hereafter referred to as *AMG*), plate facing 150 and 151, note 1.

way, I went forward out of sight; and sitting down, I read the twenty-second chapter of the Revelations: "He showed me a river of water, clear as crystal, proceeding out of the throne of God and the Lamb, etc." And in reading it my mind was drawn to seek after that pure habitation which I then believed God had prepared for his servants. The place where I sat and the sweetness that attended my mind remains fresh in my memory.

This and the like gracious visitations had that effect upon me, that when boys used ill language it troubled me, and through the continued mercies of God I was preserved from it. The pious instructions of my parents were often fresh in my mind when I happened amongst wicked children, and was of use to me. My parents, having a large family of children, used frequently on First Days after meeting to put us to read in the Holy Scriptures or some religious books, one after another, the rest sitting by without much conversation, which I have since often thought was a good practice. From what I had read and heard, I believed there had been in past ages people who walked in uprightness before God in a degree exceeding any that I knew, or heard of, now living; and the apprehension of there being less steadiness and firmness amongst people in this age than in past ages often troubled me while I was a child.

I had a dream about the ninth year of my age as follows: I saw the moon rise near the west and run a regular course eastward, so swift that in about a quarter of an hour she reached our meridian, when there descended from her a small cloud on a direct line to the earth, which lighted on a pleasant green about twenty yards from the door of my father's house (in which I thought I stood) and was immediately turned into a beautiful green tree. The moon appeared to run on with equal swiftness and soon set in the east, at which time the sun arose at the place where it commonly does in the summer, and shining with full radiance in a serene air, it appeared as pleasant a morning as ever I saw.

All this time I stood still in the door in an awful[2] frame of mind, and I observed that as heat increased by the rising sun, it wrought so powerfully on the little green tree that the leaves gradually withered; and before noon

---

2. "Awful. Inspiring awe. It does not mean 'terrible' or 'bad.'" Phillips P. Moulton, ed., *The Journal and Major Essays of John Woolman*, 314 (hereafter referred to as *PM*).

it appeared dry and dead. There then appeared a being, small of size, full of strength and resolution, moving swift from the north, southward, called a sun worm.

Another thing remarkable in my childhood was that once, going to a neighbour's house, I saw on the way a robin sitting on her nest; and as I came near she went off, but having young ones, flew about and with many cries expressed her concern for them. I stood and threw stones at her, till one striking her, she fell down dead. At first I was pleased with the exploit, but after a few minutes was seized with horror, as having in a sportive way killed an innocent creature while she was careful for her young. I beheld her lying dead and thought those young ones for which she was so careful must now perish for want of their dam to nourish them; and after some painful considerations on the subject, I climbed up the tree, took all the young birds and killed them, supposing that better than to leave them to pine away and die miserably, and believed in this case that Scripture proverb was fulfilled, "The tender mercies of the wicked are cruel" [Prov. 12:10]. I then went on my errand, but for some hours could think of little else but the cruelties I had committed, and was much troubled. Thus he whose tender mercies are over all his works hath placed a principle in the human mind which incites to exercise goodness toward every living creature; and this being singly attended to, people become tender-hearted and sympathizing, but being frequently and totally rejected, the mind shuts itself up in a contrary disposition.

About the twelfth year of my age, my father being abroad, my mother reproved me for some misconduct, to which I made an undutiful reply; and the next First Day as I was with my father returning from meeting, he told me he understood I had behaved amiss to my mother and advised me to be more careful in future. I knew myself blameable, and in shame and confusion remained silent. Being thus awakened to a sense of my wickedness, I felt remorse in my mind, and getting home I retired and prayed to the Lord to forgive me, and do not remember that I ever after that spoke unhandsomely to either of my parents, however foolish in other things.

Having attained the age of sixteen years, I began to love wanton company, and though I was preserved from profane language or scandalous conduct, still I perceived a plant in me which produced much wild grapes. Yet my merciful Father forsook me not utterly, but at times through his grace I was brought seriously to consider my ways, and the sight of my backsliding affected me with sorrow. But for want of rightly attending to the reproofs of instruction, vanity was added to vanity, and repentance to repentance; upon the whole my mind was more and more alienated from the Truth,[3] and I hastened toward destruction. While I meditate on the gulf toward which I travelled and reflect on my youthful disobedience, for these things I weep; mine eye runneth down with water.

Advancing in age the number of my acquaintance increased, and thereby my way grew more difficult. Though I had heretofore found comfort in reading the Holy Scriptures and thinking on heavenly things, I was now estranged therefrom. I knew I was going from the flock of Christ and had no resolution to return; hence serious reflections were uneasy to me and youthful vanities and diversions my greatest pleasure. Running in this road I found many like myself, and we associated in that which is reverse to true friendship.

But in this swift race it pleased God to visit me with sickness, so that I doubted of recovering. And then did darkness, horror, and amazement with full force seize me, even when my pain and distress of body was very great. I thought it would have been better for me never to have had a being than to see the day which I now saw. I was filled with confusion, and in great affliction both of mind and body I lay and bewailed myself. I had not confidence to lift up my cries to God, whom I had thus offended, but in a deep sense of my great folly I was humbled before him, and at length that Word which is as a fire and a hammer broke and dissolved my rebellious heart. And then my cries were put up in contrition, and in the multitude of his mercies I found inward relief, and felt a close engagement that if he was pleased to restore my health, I might walk humbly before him.

After my recovery this exercise remained with me a considerable time;[4] but by degrees giving way to youthful vanities, they gained strength, and

---

3. "Truth (capitalized). Ultimate spiritual reality; divinity. This usage is to be distinguished from reference to particular truths, such as creedal affirmations." *PM*, 314.

4. "Exercise. Inner turmoil; concern; awareness of a burden or obligation. The word has many nuances of meaning, all of which concern intellectual or spiritual, as distinguished from physical, exertion." *PM*, 314.

getting with wanton young people I lost ground. The Lord had been very gracious and spoke peace to me in the time of my distress, and I now most ungratefully turned again to folly, on which account at times I felt sharp reproof but did not get low enough to cry for help. I was not so hardy as to commit things scandalous, but to exceed in vanity[5] and promote mirth was my chief study. Still I retained a love and esteem for pious people, and their company brought an awe upon me.

My dear parents several times admonished me in the fear of the Lord, and their admonition entered into my heart and had a good effect for a season, but not getting deep enough to pray rightly, the tempter when he came found entrance. I remember once, having spent a part of the day in wantonness, as I went to bed at night there lay in a window near my bed a Bible, which I opened, and first cast my eye on the text, "We lie down in our shame, and our confusion covers us" [Jer. 3:25]. This I knew to be my case, and meeting with so unexpected a reproof, I was somewhat affected with it and went to bed under remorse of conscience, which I soon cast off again.

Thus time passed on; my heart was replenished with mirth and wantonness, while pleasing scenes of vanity were presented to my imagination till I attained the age of eighteen years, near which time I felt the judgments of God in my soul like a consuming fire, and looking over my past life the prospect was moving. I was often sad and longed to be delivered from those vanities; then again my heart was strongly inclined to them, and there was in me a sore conflict. At times I turned to folly, and then again sorrow and confusion took hold of me. In a while I resolved totally to leave off some of my vanities, but there was a secret reserve in my heart of the more refined part of them, and I was not low enough to find true peace. Thus for some months I had great trouble, there remaining in me an unsubjected will which rendered my labours fruitless, till at length through the merciful continuance of heavenly visitations I was made to bow down in spirit before the Lord.

I remember one evening I had spent some time in reading a pious author, and walking out alone I humbly prayed to the Lord for his help, that I might be delivered from all those vanities which so ensnared me. Thus being brought low, he helped me; and as I learned to bear the cross I felt

---

5. "For 'vanity' MS. C substitutes 'the art of foolish jesting.'" *PM*, 26, note 16.

refreshment to come from his presence; but not keeping in that strength which gave victory, I lost ground again, the sense of which greatly affected me; and I sought deserts and lonely places and there with tears did confess my sins to God and humbly craved help of him. And I may say with reverence he was near to me in my troubles, and in those times of humiliation opened my ear to discipline.

I was now led to look seriously at the means by which I was drawn from the pure Truth, and learned this: that if I would live in the life which the faithful servants of God lived in, I must not go into company as heretofore in my own will, but all the cravings of sense must be governed by a divine principle. In times of sorrow and abasement these instructions were sealed upon me, and I felt the power of Christ prevail over selfish desires, so that I was preserved in a good degree of steadiness. And being young and believing at that time that a single life was best for me, I was strengthened to keep from such company as had often been a snare to me.

I kept steady to meetings, spent First Days after noon chiefly in reading the Scriptures and other good books, and was early convinced in my mind that true religion consisted in an inward life, wherein the heart doth love and reverence God the Creator and learn to exercise true justice and goodness, not only toward all men but also toward the brute creatures; that as the mind was moved on an inward principle to love God as an invisible, incomprehensible being, on the same principle it was moved to love him in all his manifestations in the visible world; that as by his breath the flame of life was kindled in all animal and sensitive creatures, to say we love God as unseen and at the same time exercise cruelty toward the least creature moving by his life, or by life derived from him, was a contradiction in itself.

I found no narrowness respecting sects and opinions, but believed that sincere, upright-hearted people in every Society who truly loved God were accepted of him.

As I lived under the cross and simply followed the openings[6] of Truth, my mind from day to day was more enlightened; my former acquaintance was left to judge of me as they would, for I found it safest for me to live in private and keep these things sealed up in my own breast.

---

6. "Opening. Revelation, guidance, leading." *PM,* 314.

While I silently ponder on that change wrought in me, I find no language equal to it nor any means to convey to another a clear idea of it. I looked upon the works of God in this visible creation and an awfulness covered me; my heart was tender and often contrite, and a universal love to my fellow creatures increased in me. This will be understood by such who have trodden in the same path. Some glances of real beauty may be seen in their faces who dwell in true meekness. There is a harmony in the sound of that voice to which divine love gives utterance, and some appearance of right order in their temper and conduct whose passions are fully regulated. Yet all these do not fully show forth that inward life to such who have not felt it, but this white stone and new name is known rightly to such only who have it.

Now though I had been thus strengthened to bear the cross, I still found myself in great danger, having many weaknesses attending me and strong temptations to wrestle with, in the feeling whereof I frequently withdrew into private places and often with tears besought the Lord to help me, whose gracious ear was open to my cry.

All this time I lived with my parents and wrought on the plantation, and having had schooling pretty well for a planter, I used to improve in winter evenings and other leisure times. And being now in the twenty-first year of my age, a man in much business shopkeeping and baking asked me if I would hire with him to tend shop and keep books. I acquainted my father with the proposal, and after some deliberation it was agreed for me to go.

At home I had lived retired, and now having a prospect of being much in the way of company, I felt frequent and fervent cries in my heart to God, the Father of Mercies, that he would preserve me from all taint and corruption, that in this more public employ I might serve him, my gracious Redeemer, in that humility and self-denial with which I had been in a small degree exercised in a very private life.

The man who employed me furnished a shop in Mount Holly, about five miles from my father's house and six from his own, and there I lived alone and tended his shop. Shortly after my settlement here I was visited by several young people, my former acquaintance, who knew not but vanities would be as agreeable to me now as ever; and at these times I cried to the Lord in secret for wisdom and strength, for I felt myself encompassed with difficulties and had fresh occasion to bewail the follies of time past in contracting a familiarity with a libertine people. And as I had now left my father's house outwardly,[7] I found my Heavenly Father to be merciful to me beyond what I can express.

By day I was much amongst people and had many trials to go through, but in evenings I was mostly alone and may with thankfulness acknowledge that in those times the spirit of supplication was often poured upon me, under which I was frequently exercised and felt my strength renewed.

In a few months after I came here, my master bought several Scotch menservants from on board a vessel and brought them to Mount Holly to sell, one of which was taken sick and died. The latter part of his sickness he, being delirious, used to curse and swear most sorrowfully, and after he was buried I was left to sleep alone the next night in the same chamber where he died. I perceived in me a timorousness. I knew, however, I had not injured the man but assisted in taking care of him according to my capacity, and was not free to ask anyone on that occasion to sleep with me. Nature was feeble, but every trial was a fresh incitement to give myself up wholly to the service of God, for I found no helper like him in times of trouble.

After a while my former acquaintance gave over expecting me as one of their company, and I began to be known to some whose conversation was helpful to me. And now, as I had experienced the love of God through Jesus Christ to redeem me from many pollutions and to be a succour to me through a sea of conflicts, with which no person was fully acquainted, and as my heart was often enlarged in this heavenly principle, I felt a tender compassion for the youth who remained entangled in snares like those which had entangled me. From one month to another this love and tenderness increased, and my mind was more strongly engaged for the good of my fellow creatures.

I went to meetings in an awful frame of mind and endeavoured to be inwardly acquainted with the language of the True Shepherd. And one day being under a strong exercise of spirit, I stood up and said some words in a meeting, but not keeping close to the divine opening, I said more than was required of me; and being soon sensible of my error, I was afflicted in mind

---

7. "Outward. External; material; physical; worldly—the opposite of internal or spiritual." *PM,* 314.

some weeks without any light or comfort, even to that degree that I could take satisfaction in nothing. I remembered God and was troubled, and in the depth of my distress he had pity upon me and sent the Comforter. I then felt forgiveness for my offense, and my mind became calm and quiet, being truly thankful to my gracious Redeemer for his mercies. And after this, feeling the spring of divine love opened and a concern to speak, I said a few words in a meeting, in which I found peace. This I believe was about six weeks from the first time, and as I was thus humbled and disciplined under the cross, my understanding became more strengthened to distinguish the language of the pure Spirit which inwardly moves upon the heart and taught [me] to wait in silence sometimes many weeks together, until I felt that rise which prepares the creature to stand like a trumpet through which the Lord speaks to his flock.

From an inward purifying, and steadfast abiding under it, springs a lively operative desire for the good of others. All faithful people are not called to the public ministry, but whoever are, are called to minister of that which they have tasted and handled spiritually. The outward modes of worship are various, but wherever men are true ministers of Jesus Christ it is from the operation of his spirit upon their hearts, first purifying them and thus giving them a feeling sense of the conditions of others. This truth was early fixed in my mind, and I was taught to watch the pure opening and to take heed lest while I was standing to speak, my own will should get uppermost and cause me to utter words from worldly wisdom and depart from the channel of the true gospel ministry.

In the management of my outward affairs I may say with thankfulness I found Truth to be my support, and I was respected in my master's family, who came to live in Mount Holly within two year after my going there.

About the twenty-third year of my age, I had many fresh and heavenly openings in respect to the care and providence of the Almighty over his creatures in general, and over man as the most noble amongst those which are visible. And being clearly convinced in my judgment that to place my whole trust in God was best for me, I felt renewed engagements that in all things I might act on an inward principle of virtue and pursue worldly business no further than as Truth opened my way therein.

About the time called Christmas I observed many people from the country and dwellers in town who, resorting to the public houses,[8] spent their time in drinking and vain sports, tending to corrupt one another, on which account I was much troubled. At one house in particular there was much disorder, and I believed it was a duty laid on me to go and speak to the master of that house. I considered I was young and that several elderly Friends in town had opportunity to see these things, and though I would gladly have been excused, yet I could not feel my mind clear.

The exercise was heavy, and as I was reading what the Almighty said to Ezekiel respecting his duty as a watchman, the matter was set home more clearly; and then with prayer and tears I besought the Lord for his assistance, who in loving-kindness gave me a resigned heart. Then at a suitable opportunity I went to the public house, and seeing the man amongst a company, I went to him and told him I wanted to speak with him; so we went aside, and there in the fear and dread of the Almighty I expressed to him what rested on my mind, which he took kindly, and afterward showed more regard to me than before. In a few years after, he died middle-aged, and I often thought that had I neglected my duty in that case it would have given me great trouble, and I was humbly thankful to my gracious Father, who had supported me herein.

My employer, having a Negro woman, sold her and directed me to write a bill of sale, the man being waiting who bought her. The thing was sudden, and though the thoughts of writing an instrument of slavery for one of my fellow creatures felt uneasy,[9] yet I remembered I was hired by the year, that it was my master who directed me to do it, and that it was an elderly man, a member of our society who bought her; so through weakness I gave way and wrote it, but at the executing it, I was so afflicted in my mind that I said before my master and the Friend that I believed slavekeeping to be a practice inconsistent with the Christian religion. This in some degree abated my uneasiness, yet as often as I reflected seriously upon it I thought I should have been clearer if I had desired to be excused from it as a thing

---

8.   Public house. A pub or tavern.

9.   Uneasy. Not at ease with one's conscience; not inwardly free. Hence, "easy" does not necessarily imply "without difficulty."

against my conscience, for such it was. And some time after this a young man of our Society[10] spake to me to write an instrument of slavery, he having lately taken a Negro into his house. I told him I was not easy to write it, for though many kept slaves in our Society, as in others I still believed the practice was not right, and desired to be excused from writing [it]. I spoke to him in good will, and he told me that keeping slaves was not altogether agreeable to his mind, but that the slave being a gift made to his wife, he had accepted of her.

from Chapter 2
1746

...We left our province on the 12th day, 3rd month, 1746, and had several meetings in the upper part of Chester County and near Lancaster, in some of which the love of Christ prevailed, uniting us together in his service. Then we crossed the River Susquehanna and had several meetings in a new settlement called the Red Lands, the oldest of which did not exceed ten years. It is the poorer sort of people that commonly begin to improve remote deserts. With a small stock[11] they have houses to build, lands to clear and fence, corn to raise, clothes to provide, and children to educate, that Friends who visit such way well sympathize with them in their hardships in the wilderness; and though the best entertainment such can give may seem coarse to some who are used to cities or old settled places, it becomes the disciples of Christ to be content with it. Our hearts were sometimes enlarged in the love of our Heavenly Father amongst these people, and the sweet influence of his spirit supported us through some difficulties. To him be the praise.

We passed on to Monocacy, Fairfax, Hopewell, and Shenandoah and had meetings, some of which were comfortable[12] and edifying. From Shenandoah

---

10. "Society (capitalized). Religious sect or denomination; usually refers to the Society of Friends." *PM,* 314.

11. "Stock. Supply of money or capital; treasury." *PM,* 314.

12. "Comfortable. Satisfactory; fruitful; enriching. Spiritual or inward comfort in this sense is that occasioned by an experience according with one's higher values or conscience,

we set off in the afternoon for the old settlements of Friends in Virginia, and the first night we, with our pilot, lodged in the woods, our horses feeding near us. But he being poorly provided with a horse, and we young and having good horses, [we] were free the next day to part with him and did so. And in two days beside the first afternoon we reached to our friend John Cheagles in Virginia. So we took the meetings in our way through Virginia, were in some degree baptized[13] into a feeling sense of the conditions of the people, and our exercise in general was more painful in these old settlements than it had been amongst the back inhabitants. But through the goodness of our Heavenly Father, the well of living waters was at times opened, to our encouragement and the refreshment of the sincere-hearted.

We went on to Perquimans River in North Carolina, had several meetings which were large, and found some openness in those parts and a hopeful appearance amongst the young people. So we turned again to Virginia and attended most of the meetings which we had not been at before, labouring amongst Friends in the love of Jesus Christ as ability was given, and thence went to the mountains up James River to a new settlement and had several meetings amongst the people, some of whom had lately joined in membership with our Society. In our journeying to and fro, we found some honest-hearted Friends who appeared to be concerned for the cause of Truth among a backsliding people.

We crossed from Virginia over the river Potomac at Hoe's Ferry and made a general visit to the meetings of Friends on the western shore of Maryland and were at their Quarterly Meeting. We had some hard labour amongst them, endeavouring to discharge our duties honestly as way opened in the love of Truth. And thence taking sundry meetings in our way, we passed homeward, where through the favour of divine providence we reached the 16th day, 6th month, 1746; and I may say that through the assistance of the Holy Spirit, which mortifies selfish desires, my companion and I travelled in harmony and parted in the nearness of true brotherly love.

---

but not necessarily comfortable in the physical sense." *PM,* 314.

13. "Baptize. To initiate; to acquaint; to make aware; to enrich spiritually—generally implying that the awareness or enrichment is brought about through a trying experience." *PM,* 314.

Two things were remarkable to me in this journey. First, in regard to my entertainment: When I eat, drank, and lodged free-cost with people who lived in ease on the hard labour of their slaves, I felt uneasy; and as my mind was inward to the Lord, I found, from place to place, this uneasiness return upon me at times through the whole visit. Where the masters bore a good share of the burden and lived frugal, so that their servants were well provided for and their labour moderate, I felt more easy; but where they lived in a costly way and laid heavy burdens on their slaves, my exercise was often great, and I frequently had conversation with them in private concerning it. Secondly, this trade of importing them from their native country being much encouraged amongst them and the white people and their children so generally living without much labour was frequently the subject of my serious thoughts. And I saw in these southern provinces so many vices and corruptions increased by this trade and this way of life that it appeared to me as a dark gloominess hanging over the land; and though now many willingly run into it, yet in future the consequence will be grievous to posterity! I express it as it hath appeared to me, not at once nor twice, but as a matter fixed on my mind....

from Chapter 3
1755–1756

...About this time an ancient man of good esteem in the neighbourhood came to my house to get his will wrote. He had young Negroes, and I asking him privately how he purposed to dispose of them, he told me. I then said, "I cannot write thy will without breaking my own peace," and respectfully gave him my reasons for it. He signified that he had a choice that I should have wrote it, but as I could not consistent with my conscience, he did not desire it, and so he got it wrote by some other person. And a few years after, there being great alterations in his family, he came again to get me to write his will. His Negroes were yet young, and his son, to whom he intended to give them, was since he first spoke to me, from a libertine become a sober young man; and he supposed that I would have been free on that account to write it. We had much friendly talk on the subject and then deferred it, and a few days after, he came again and directed their freedom, and so I wrote his will.

Near the time the last-mentioned friend first spoke to me, a neighbour received a bad bruise in his body and sent for me to bleed him, which being done he desired me to write his will. I took notes, and amongst other things he told me to which of his children he gave his young Negro. I considered the pain and distress he was in and knew not how it would end, so I wrote his will, save only that part concerning his slave, and carrying it to his bedside read it to him and then told him in a friendly way that I could not write any instruments by which my fellow creatures were made slaves, without bringing trouble on my own mind. I let him know that I charged nothing for what I had done and desired to be excused from doing the other part in the way he proposed. Then we had a serious conference on the subject, and at length, he agreeing to set her free, I finished his will....

Until the year 1756 I continued to retail goods, besides following my trade as a tailor, about which time I grew uneasy on account of my business growing too cumbersome. I began with selling trimmings for garments and from thence proceeded to sell clothes and linens, and at length having got a considerable shop of goods, my trade increased every year and the road to large business appeared open; but I felt a stop in my mind.

Through the mercies of the Almighty I had in a good degree learned to be content with a plain way of living. I had but a small family, that on serious consideration I believed Truth did not require me to engage in much cumbrous affairs. It had been my general practice to buy and sell things really useful. Things that served chiefly to please the vain mind in people I was not easy to trade in, seldom did it, and whenever I did I found it weaken me as a Christian.

The increase of business became my burden, for though my natural inclination was toward merchandise, yet I believed Truth required me to live more free from outward cumbers, and there was now a strife in my mind between the two; and in this exercise my prayers were put up to the Lord, who graciously heard me and gave me a heart resigned to his holy will. Then I lessened my outward business, and as I had opportunity told my customers of my intentions that they might consider what shop to turn to, and so in a while wholly laid down merchandise, following my trade as a tailor, myself only, having no apprentice. I also had a nursery of apple trees, in which I employed some of my time—hoeing grafting, trimming, and inoculating.

In merchandise it is the custom where I lived to sell chiefly on credit, and poor people often get in debt, and when payment is expected, not having wherewith to pay, their creditors often sue for it at law. Having often observed occurrences of this kind, I found it good for me to advise poor people to take such goods as were most useful and not costly....

from Chapter 4
1757

The 13th day, 2nd month, 1757. Being then in good health and abroad with Friends visiting families, I lodged at a Friend's house in Burlington, and going to bed about the time usual with me, I woke in the night and my meditations as I lay were on the goodness and mercy of the Lord, in a sense whereof my heart was contrite. After this I went to sleep again, and sleeping a short time I awoke. It was yet dark and no appearance of day nor moonshine, and as I opened my eyes I saw a light in my chamber at the apparent distance of five feet, about nine inches diameter, of a clear, easy brightness and near the center the most radiant. As I lay still without any surprise looking upon it, words were spoken to my inward ear which filled my whole inward man. They were not the effect of thought nor any conclusion in relation to the appearance, but as the language of the Holy One spoken in my mind. The words were, "Certain Evidence of Divine Truth," and were again repeated exactly in the same manner, whereupon the light disappeared....

Conduct is more convincing than language, and where people by their actions manifest that the slave trade is not so disagreeable to their principles but that it may be encouraged, there is not a sound uniting with some Friends who visit them.

The prospect of so weighty a work, and being so distinguished from many who I esteemed before myself, brought me very low, and such were the conflicts of my soul that I had a near sympathy with the prophet in the time of his weakness, when he said, "If thou deal thus with me, kill me I pray thee out of hand, if I have found favour in thy sight" [Num. 11:15]. But I soon saw that this proceeded from the want of a full resignation to him.

Many were the afflictions which attended me, and in great abasement with many tears, my cries were to the Almighty for his gracious and fatherly assistance; and then after a time of deep trial, I was favoured to understand the state mentioned by the Psalmist more clearly than ever I had before, to wit: "My soul is even as a weaned child" [Ps. 131:2]. Being thus helped to sink down into resignation, I felt a deliverance from that tempest in which I had been sorely exercised, and in calmness of mind went forward, trusting that the Lord, as I faithfully attended to him, would be a counsellor to me in all difficulties, and that by his strength I should be enabled even to leave money with the members of [the] Society where I had entertainment when I found that omitting of it would obstruct that work to which I believed he had called me. And as I copy this after my return, I may here add that oftentimes I did so under a sense of duty.

The way in which I did it was thus: When I expected soon to leave a Friend's house where I had entertainment, if I believed that I should not keep clear from the gain of oppression without leaving money, I spoke to one of the heads of the family privately and desired them to accept of them pieces of silver and give them to such of their Negroes as they believed would make the best use of them; and at other times I gave them to the Negroes myself, as the way looked clearest to me. As I expected this before I came out, I had provided a large number of small pieces, and thus offering them to some who appeared to be wealthy people was a trial both to me and them. But the fear of the Lord so covered me at times that way was made easier than I expected, and few if any manifested any resentment at the offer, and most of them after some talk accepted of them....

from Chapter 5
1758

...The Monthly Meeting of Philadelphia having been under a concern on account of some Friends who this summer, 1758, had bought Negro slaves, the said meeting moved it in their Quarterly Meeting to have the minute reconsidered in the Yearly Meeting which was made last on that subject.

And the said Quarterly Meeting appointed a committee to consider it and report to their next, which committee having met once and adjourned, and I, going to Philadelphia to meet a committee of the Yearly Meeting, was in town the evening on which the Quarterly Meeting's committee met the second time, and finding an inclination to sit with them, was admitted; and Friends had a weighty conference on the subject. And soon after their next Quarterly Meeting I heard that the case was coming to our Yearly Meeting, which brought a weighty exercise upon me, and under a sense of my own infirmities and the great danger I felt of turning aside from perfect purity, my mind was often drawn to retire alone and put up my prayers to the Lord that he would be graciously pleased to strengthen me, that setting aside all views of self-interest and the friendship of this world, I might stand fully resigned to his holy will.

In this Yearly Meeting several weighty matters were considered, and toward the last, that in relation to dealing with persons who purchase slaves. During the several sittings of the said meeting, my mind was frequently covered with inward prayer, and I could say with David that tears were my meat day and night [Ps. 42:3]. The case of slavekeeping lay heavy upon me, nor did I find any engagement to speak directly to any other matter before the meeting. Now when this case was opened, several faithful Friends spake weightily thereto, with which I was comforted, and feeling a concern to cast in my mite, I said in substance as follows:

> In the difficulties attending us in this life, nothing is more precious than the mind of Truth inwardly manifested, and it is my earnest desire that in this weighty matter we may be so truly humbled as to be favoured with a clear understanding of the mind of Truth and follow it; this would be of more advantage to the Society than any mediums which are not in the clearness of divine wisdom. The case is difficult to some who have them, but if such set aside all self-interest and come to be weaned from the desire of getting estates, or even from holding them together when Truth requires the contrary, I believe way will open that they will know how to steer through those difficulties.

Many Friends appeared to be deeply bowed under the weight of the work and manifested much firmness in their love to the cause of truth and universal righteousness in the earth. And though none did openly justify the practice of slavekeeping in general, yet some appeared concerned lest the meeting should go into such measures as might give uneasiness to many brethren, alleging that if Friends patiently continued under the exercise, the Lord in time to come might open a way for the deliverance of these people. And I, finding an engagement to speak, said:

> My mind is often led to consider the purity of the Divine Being and the justice of his judgments, and herein my soul is covered with awfulness. I cannot omit to hint of some cases where people have not been treated with the purity of justice, and the event hath been melancholy.

> Many slaves on this continent are oppressed, and their cries have reached the ears of the Most High! Such is the purity and certainty of his judgments that he cannot be partial in our favour. In infinite love and goodness he hath opened our understandings from one time to another concerning our duty toward this people, and it is not a time for delay.

> Should we now be sensible of what he requires of us, and through a respect to the private interest of some persons or through a regard to some friendships which do not stand on an immutable foundation, neglect to do our duty in firmness and constancy, still waiting for some extraordinary means to bring about their deliverance, it may be that by terrible things in righteousness God may answer us in this matter.

Many faithful brethren laboured with great firmness, and the love of Truth in a good degree prevailed. Several Friends who had Negroes expressed their desire that a rule might be made to deal with such Friends as offenders who bought slaves in future. To this it was answered that the root of this evil would never be effectually struck at until a thorough search was made into the circumstances of such Friends who kept Negroes, in regard to the righteousness of their motives in keeping them, that impartial justice might be administered throughout.

Several Friends expressed their desire that a visit might be made to such Friends who kept slaves, and many Friends declared that they believed liberty was the Negro's right, to which at length no opposition was made publicly, so that a minute was made more full on that subject than any heretofore and the names of several Friends entered who were free to join in a visit to such who kept slaves.[14]

from Chapter 7
1760

...We visited the meetings in those parts and were measurably baptized into a feeling of the state of the Society, and in bowedness of spirit went to the Yearly Meeting at Newport, where I understood that a large number of slaves were imported from Africa and then on sale by a member of our Society. At this meeting we met with John Storer from England, Elizabeth Shipley, Ann Gauntt, Hannah Foster, and Mercy Redman from our parts, all ministers of the gospel, of whose company I was glad.[15] At this time I

14. A committee was established for the visitation of friends who owned slaves--a decision that opened the way for the Yearly Meeting to take more restrictive positions against Quaker slave owners. Without fully explaining the significance of this committee, chapter 6 begins by describing Woolman's active service on the committee. In its opening paragraphs, Woolman observes that he joined with "friends Daniel Stanton and John Scarborough in visiting Friends who had slaves." *PM,* 94; The other members of the visitation committee were John Churchman and John Sykes. These visits would continue for the next five years. Although the Yearly Meeting of 1758 was not ready to disown those who continued to buy and sell slaves, the visitation committee had the effect of maintaining pressure on those involved in the slave trade. Hugh Barbour and J. William Frost, *The Quakers,* 123.

15. See letters concerning this journey to the New England Yearly Meeting of 1760 in Selected Letters in this *Source Book.* Also, compare Mercy Redman's comments on the journey recorded in her journal in "Related Writings by Contemporaries." One might argue that her perspective is quite different from Woolman's.

had a feeling of the condition of Habakkuk as thus expressed: "When I heard, my belly trembled, my lips quivered, my appetite failed, and I grew outwardly weak. I trembled in myself that I might rest in the day of trouble" [Hab. 3:16]. I had many cogitations and was sorely distressed.

I was desirous that Friends might petition the Legislature to use their endeavours to discourage the future importation of them, for I saw that this trade was a great evil and tended to multiply troubles and bring distresses on the people in those parts, for whose welfare my heart was deeply concerned at this time. But I perceived several difficulties in regard to petitioning, and such was the exercise of my mind that I had thought of endeavouring to get an opportunity to speak a few words in the House of Assembly, they being then sitting in town. This exercise came upon me in the afternoon on the second day of the Yearly Meeting,[16] and going to bed I got no sleep till my mind was wholly resigned therein; and in the morning I inquired of a Friend how long the Assembly were likely to continue sitting, who told me they were expected to be prorogued that day or the next.

As I was desirous to attend the business of the meeting and perceived the Assembly were likely to depart before the business was over, after considerable exercise, humbly seeking to the Lord for instruction, my mind settled to attend on the business of the meeting, on the last day of which I had prepared a short essay of a petition to be presented to the Legislature if way opened. And having understood there were men appointed by that Yearly Meeting to speak with men in authority in cases relating to the Society, I opened my mind to several of them and showed them the essay I had made, and afterward opened the case in the meeting for business, in substance as follows:

---

16. The New England Yearly Meeting of 1760 resisted major change on the slave issue partly because significant leaders still owned slaves. Thomas Richardson, the clerk of New England Yearly Meeting from 1728–1760, was himself active in the slave trade. Barbour and Frost, 121; Although change came slowly, Woolman's visit may have been a significant turning point. Sydney V. James, *A People Among Peoples: Quaker Benevolence in Eighteenth-Century America*, 220–21.

I have been under a concern for some time on account of the great number of slaves which are imported into this colony. I am aware that it is a tender point to speak to, but apprehend I am not clear in the sight of heaven without speaking to it. I have prepared an essay of a petition proposed, if way open, to be presented to the Legislature, and what I have to propose to this meeting is that some Friends may be named to walk aside and look over it, and report whether they believe it suitable to be read in this meeting. If they should think well of reading it, it will remain for the meeting, after hearing it, to consider whether to take any further notice of it as a meeting or not.

After a short conference some Friends went out and, looking over it, expressed their willingness to have it read, which being done, many expressed their unity with the proposal, and some signified that to have the subjects of the petition enlarged upon and to be signed out of meeting by such who were free would be more suitable than to do it there. Though I expected at first that if it was done, it would be in that way, yet such was the exercise of my mind that to move it in the hearing of Friends when assembled appeared to me as a duty, for my heart yearned toward the inhabitants of these parts, believing that by this trade there had been an increase of unquietness amongst them and the way made easy for the spreading of a spirit opposite to that meekness and humility which is a sure resting place for the soul, and that the continuance of this trade would not only render their healing more difficult but increase their malady. Having thus far proceeded, I felt easy to leave the essay amongst Friends, for them to proceed in it as they believed best.

And now an exercise revived on my mind in relation to lotteries, which were common in those parts. I had once moved it in a former sitting of this meeting, when arguments were used in favour of Friends being held excused who were only concerned in such lotteries as were agreeable to law; and now on moving it again, it was opposed as before, but the hearts of some solid Friends appeared to be united to discourage the practice amongst their members, and the matter was zealously handled by some on both sides. In this debate it appeared very clear to me that the spirit of lotteries was a spirit of selfishness, which tended to confusion and darkness of understanding, and that pleading for it in our meetings, set apart for the Lord's work, was not right. And in the heat of zeal, I once made reply to what an ancient Friend said, which when I sat down I saw that my words were not enough seasoned with charity, and after this I spake no more on the subject.

At length a minute was made, a copy of which was agreed to be sent to their several Quarterly Meetings, inciting Friends to labour to discourage the practice amongst all professing with us.

Some time after this minute was made I, remaining uneasy with the manner of my speaking to an ancient Friend, could not see my way clear to conceal my uneasiness, but was concerned that I might say nothing to weaken the cause in which I had laboured. And then after some close exercise and hearty repentance for that I had not attended closely to the safe guide, I stood up and, reciting the passage, acquainted Friends that though I dare not go from what I had said as to the matter, yet I was uneasy with the manner of my speaking, as believing milder language would have been better. As this was uttered in some degree of creaturely abasement, it appeared to have a good savor amongst us, after a warm debate.

The Yearly Meeting being now over, there yet remained on my mind a secret, though heavy, exercise in regard to some leading active members about Newport being in the practice of slavekeeping. This I mentioned to two ancient Friends who came out of the country, and proposed to them, if way opened, to have some conversation with those Friends; and thereupon one of those country Friends and I consulted one of the most noted elders who had them, and he in a respectful manner encouraged me to proceed to clear myself of what lay upon me. Now I had near the beginning of the Yearly Meeting a private conference with this said elder and his wife concerning theirs, so that the way seemed clear to me to advise with him about the way of proceeding. I told him I was free to have a conference with them all together in a private house, or if he believed they would take it unkind to be asked to come together and to be spoke with one in the hearing of another, I was free to spend some time among them and visit them all in their own houses. He expressed his liking to the first proposal, not doubting their willingness to come together, and as I proposed a visit to only ministers, elders, and overseers, he named some others whom he desired might be present also; and as a careful messenger was wanted to acquaint them in a proper manner, he offered to go to all their houses to open the matter to them, and did so.

About the eighth hour the next morning we met in the meeting house chamber, and the last-mentioned country Friend, also my companion and John Storer with us. Then after a short time of retirement, I acquainted them with the steps I had taken in procuring that meeting and opened the concern I was under, and so we proceeded to a free conference upon the subject. My exercise was heavy and I was deeply bowed in spirit before the Lord, who was pleased to favour with the seasoning virtue of Truth, which wrought a tenderness amongst us, and the subject was mutually handled in a calm and peaceable spirit. And at length feeling my mind released from that burden which I had been under, I took my leave of them in a good degree of satisfaction, and by the tenderness they manifested in regard to the practice and the concern several of them expressed in relation to disposing of them after their decease, I believed that a good exercise was spreading amongst them; and I am humbly thankful to God, who supported my mind and preserved me in a good degree of resignation through these trials.

Thou who sometimes travels in the work of the ministry and art made very welcome by thy friends seest many tokens of their satisfaction in having thee for their guest. It's good for thee to dwell deep, that thou mayest feel and understand the spirits of people. If we believe Truth points toward a conference on some subjects in a private way, it's needful for us to take heed that their kindness, their freedom, and affability do not hinder us from the Lord's work. I have seen that in the midst of kindness and smooth conduct to speak close and home to them who entertain us, on points that relate to their outward interest, is hard labour; and sometimes when I have felt Truth lead toward it, I have found myself disqualified by a superficial friendship, and as the sense thereof hath abased me and my cries have been to the Lord, so I have been humbled and made content to appear weak or as a fool for his sake, and thus a door hath opened to enter upon it.

To attempt to do the Lord's work in our own way and to speak of that which is the burden of the Word in a way easy to the natural part does not reach the bottom of the disorder. To see the failings of our friends and think hard of them, without opening that which we ought to open, and still carry a face of friendship—this tends to undermine the foundation of true unity. The office of a minister of Christ is weighty, and they who now go forth as watchmen had need to be steadily on their guard against the snares of prosperity and an outside friendship....

Being two days going to Nantucket and having been once before, I observed many shoals in their bay, which makes sailing more dangerous, especially in stormy nights. I observed also a great shoal which encloses their harbor and prevents their going in with sloops except when the tide is up. Waiting without this shoal for the rising of the tide is sometimes hazardous in storms, and waiting within they sometimes miss a fair wind. I took notice that on that small island are a great number of inhabitants and the soil not very fertile, the timber so gone that for vessels, fences, and firewood they depend chiefly on buying from the main, the cost whereof, with most of their other expenses, they depend principally upon the whale fishery to answer. I considered that if towns grew larger and lands near navigable waters more cleared, timber and wood would require more labour to get it. I understood that the whales, being much hunted, and sometimes wounded and not killed, grew more shy and difficult to come at.

I considered that the formation of the earth, the seas, the islands, bays, and rivers, the motions of the winds and great waters, which cause bars and shoals in particular places, were all the works of him who is perfect wisdom and goodness; and as people attend to his heavenly instruction and put their trust in him, he provides for them in all parts where he gives them a being....

from Chapter 8
1761–1763

...From my early acquaintance with Truth I have often felt an inward distress occasioned by the striving of a spirit in me against the operation of the Heavenly Principle, and in this circumstance have been affected with a sense of my own wretchedness, and in a mourning condition felt earnest longings for that divine help which brings the soul into true liberty. And sometimes in this state, retiring into private places, the spirit of supplication hath been given me, and under a heavenly covering have asked my gracious Father to give me a heart in all things resigned to the direction of his wisdom; and in uttering language like this, the thoughts of my wearing hats and garments dyed with a dye hurtful to them has made lasting impressions on me.

In visiting people of note in the Society who had slaves and labouring with them in brotherly love on that account, I have seen, and the sight has affected me, that a conformity to some customs distinguishable from pure wisdom has entangled many, and the desire of gain to support these customs greatly opposed the work of Truth. And sometimes when the prospect of the work before me has been such that in bowedness of spirit I have been drawn into retired places, and besought the Lord with tears that he would take me wholly under his direction and show me the way in which I ought to walk, it hath revived with strength of conviction that if I would be his faithful servant I must in all things attend to his wisdom and be teachable, and so cease from all customs contrary thereto, however used amongst religious people.

As he is the perfection of power, of wisdom, and of goodness, so I believe he hath provided that so much labour shall be necessary for men's support in this world as would, being rightly divided, be a suitable employment of their time, and that we cannot go into superfluities, or grasp after wealth in a way contrary to his wisdom, without having connection with some degree of oppression and with that spirit which leads to self-exaltation and strife, and which frequently brings calamities on countries by parties contending about their claims.

Being thus fully convinced and feeling an increasing desire to live in the spirit of peace, being often sorrowfully affected in thinking on the unquiet spirit in which wars are generally carried on, and with the miseries of many of my fellow creatures engaged therein—some suddenly destroyed, some wounded and after much pain remain cripples, some deprived of all their outward substance and reduced to want, and some carried into captivity—thinking often on these things, the use of hats and garments dyed with a dye hurtful to them and wearing more clothes in summer than are useful grew more uneasy to me, believing them to be customs which have not their foundation in pure wisdom. The apprehension of being singular[17] from my beloved friends was a strait upon me, and thus I remained in the use of some things contrary to my judgment.

And on the 31st day, fifth month, 1761, I was taken ill of a fever, and after having it near a week I was in great distress of body. And one day there was a cry raised in me that I might understand the cause why I was afflicted and improve under it, and my conformity to some customs which I believed were not right were brought to my remembrance. And in the continuation of the exercise I felt all the powers in me yield themselves up into the hands of him who gave me being and was made thankful that he had taken hold of me by his chastisement, feeling the necessity of further purifying. There was now no desire in me for health until the design of my correction was answered, and thus I lay in abasement and brokenness of spirit. And as I felt a sinking down into a calm resignation, so I felt, as in an instant, an inward healing in my nature, and from that time forward I grew better.

Though I was thus settled in mind in relation to hurtful dyes, I felt easy to wear my garments heretofore made, and so continued about nine months. Then I thought of getting a hat the natural colour of the fur, but the apprehension of being looked upon as one affecting singularity felt uneasy to me. And here I had occasion to consider that things, though small in themselves, being clearly enjoined by divine authority became great things to us, and I trusted the Lord would support me in the trials that might attend singularity while that singularity was only for his sake. On this account I was under close exercise of mind in the time of our General Spring Meeting, 1762, greatly desiring to be rightly directed. And at a time when one of my dear brethren was concerned in humble supplication, I, being then deeply bowed in spirit before the Lord, was made willing, in case I got safe home, to speak for a hat the natural colour of the fur, and did so.

In attending meetings this singularity was a trial upon me, and more especially at this time, as being in use among some who were fond of following the changeable modes of dress; and as some Friends who knew not on what motives I wore it carried shy of me, I felt my way for a time shut up

---

17. "Singular. Peculiar; odd; unusual; different." *PM*, 314.

in the ministry. And in this condition, my mind being turned toward my Heavenly Father with fervent cries that I might be preserved to walk before him in the meekness of wisdom, my heart was often tender in meetings, and I felt an inward consolation, which to me was very precious under those difficulties.

I had several dyed garments fit for use, which I believed it best to wear till I had occasion of new ones, and some Friends were apprehensive that my wearing such a hat savored of an affected singularity, and such who spoke with me in a friendly way I generally informed in a few words that I believed my wearing it was not in my own will. I had at times been sensible that a superficial friendship had been dangerous to me, and many Friends being now uneasy with me I found to be a providential kindness. And though I had an inclination to acquaint some valuable Friends with the manner of my being led into these things, yet upon a deeper thought I was for a time most easy to omit it, believing the present dispensation was profitable and trusting that if I kept my place the Lord in his own time would open the hearts of Friends toward me, since which I've had cause to admire his goodness and loving-kindness in leading about and instructing, and opening and enlarging my heart in some of our meetings....

Having many years felt love in my heart toward the natives of this land who dwell far back in the wilderness, whose ancestors were the owners and possessors of the land where we dwell, and who for a very small consideration assigned their inheritance to us, and being at Philadelphia in the 8th month, 1761, on a visit to some Friends who had slaves, I fell in company with some of those natives who lived on the east branch of the river Susquehanna at an Indian town called Wyalusing, about two hundred miles from Philadelphia. And in conversation with them by an interpreter, as also by observations on their countenance and conduct, I believed some of them were measurably acquainted with that divine power which subjects the rough and froward[18] will of the creature; and at times I felt inward drawings[19] toward a visit to

---

18. Froward. Stubbornly contrary and disobedient.

19. "Drawings. A sense of guidance or mission; a 'vocation,' usually to a particular act rather than to a lifelong occupation. Hence, to be 'drawn' is to experience this sense." *PM*, 314.

that place, of which I told none except my dear wife until it came to some ripeness.

And then in the winter, 1762, I laid it before Friends at our Monthly and Quarterly and then at our General Spring Meeting, and having the unity of Friends and being thoughtful about an Indian pilot, there came a man and three women from a little beyond that town to Philadelphia on business; and I, being informed thereof by letter, met them in town on the 5th month, 1763. And after some conversation finding they were sober people, I, by the concurrence of Friends in that place, agreed to join with them as companions in their return; and the 7th day, 5th month, following we appointed to meet at Samuel Foulke's at Richland. Now as this visit felt weighty and was performed at a time when travelling appeared perilous, so the dispensations of divine providence in preparing my mind for it have been memorable, and I believe it good for me to give some hints thereof.

After I had given up to go, the thoughts of the journey were often attended with an unusual sadness, in which times my heart was frequently turned to the Lord with inward breathings for his heavenly support, that I might not fail to follow him wheresoever he might lead me. And being at our youths' meeting at Chesterfield about a week before the time I expected to set off, was there led to speak on that prayer of our Redeemer to his Father: "I pray not that thou shouldest take them out of the world, but that thou shouldest keep them from evil" [Jn. 17:9]. And in attending to the pure openings of Truth, [I] had to mention what he elsewhere said to his Father: "I know that thou hearest me at all times" [Jn. 11:42], so that as some of his followers kept their places, and as his prayer was granted, it followed necessarily that they were kept from evil. And as some of those met with great hardships and afflictions in this world and at last suffered death by cruel men, it appears that whatever befalls men while they live in pure obedience to God, as it certainly works for their good, so it may not be considered an evil as it relates to them. As I spake on this subject my heart was much tendered and great awfulness came over me.

And then on the first day of the next week, being at our own afternoon meeting and my heart being enlarged in love, I was led to speak on the care and protection of the Lord over his people and to make mention of that passage where a band of Assyrians, endeavouring to take captive the prophet, were disappointed, and how the Psalmist said, "The angel of the Lord encampeth round about them that fear him" [Ps. 34:7]. And thus in true love and tenderness I parted from Friends, expecting the next morning to proceed on my journey, and being weary went early to bed.

And after I had been asleep a short time, I was awaked by a man calling at my door, and arising was invited to meet some Friends at a public house in our town who came from Philadelphia so late that Friends were generally gone to bed. These Friends informed me that an express arrived the last morning from Pittsburgh and brought news that the Indians had taken a fort from the English westward and slain and scalped English people in divers places, some near the said Pittsburgh, and that some elderly Friends in Philadelphia, knowing the time of my expecting to set off, had conferred together and thought good to inform me of these things before I left home, that I might consider them and proceed as I believed best. So I, going again to bed, told not my wife till morning. My heart was turned to the Lord for his heavenly instruction, and it was a humbling time to me.

When I told my dear wife she appeared to be deeply concerned about it, but in a few hours time my mind became settled in a belief that it was my duty to proceed on my journey, and she bore it with a good degree of resignation. In this conflict of spirit there were great searchings of heart and strong cries to the Lord that no motion might be in the least degree attended to but that of the pure spirit of Truth.

The subjects before-mentioned, on which I had so lately spake in public, were now very fresh before me, and I was brought inwardly to commit myself to the Lord to be disposed of as he saw good. So I took leave of my family and neighbours in much bowedness of spirit and went to our Monthly Meeting at Burlington. And after taking leave of Friends there I crossed the river, accompanied by my friends Israel and John Pemberton[20;] and parting the

---

20. "Israel Pemberton (1715–1779), James (1723–1809), and John (1727–1795). The Pemberton brothers were prominent Quakers and civic leaders in Philadelphia. They were well-educated, successful in business, and inclined toward philanthropy. During the French and Indian War they sought to establish closer and friendlier relations with the Indians. Because of their pacifism, they were arrested and imprisoned in Virginia during the Revolutionary War. Israel seems to have advised Woolman on financial matters. All

next morning with Israel, John bore me company to Samuel Foulke's, where I met the before-mentioned Indians, and we were glad to see each other.

Here my friend Benjamin Parvin[21] met me and proposed joining as a companion, we having passed some letters before on the subject. And now on his account I had a sharp trial, for as the journey appeared perilous, I thought if he went chiefly to bear me company and we should be taken captive, my having been the means of drawing him into these difficulties would add to my own afflictions. So I told him my mind freely and let him know that I was resigned to go alone, but after all, if he really believed it to be his duty to go on, I believed his company would be very comfortable to me. It was indeed a time of deep exercise, and Benjamin appeared to be so fastened to the visit that he could not be easy to leave me; so we went on, accompanied by our friends John Pemberton, and William Lightfoot of Pikeland, and lodged at Bethlehem.

And there parting with John, William and we went forward on the 9th day, 6th month, and got lodging on the floor at a house about five mile from Fort Allen. Here we parted with William, and at this place we met with an Indian trader lately come from Wyoming, and in conversation with him I perceived that many white people do often sell rum to the Indians, which I believe is a great evil. First, they being thereby deprived of the use of their reason and their spirits violently agitated, quarrels often arise which ends in mischief, and the bitterness and resentments occasioned hereby are frequently of long continuance. Again, their skins and furs, gotten through much fatigue and hard travels in hunting, with which they intended to buy clothing, these when they begin to be intoxicated they often sell at a low rate for more rum; and afterward when they suffer for want of the necessaries of life, [they] are angry with those who for the sake of gain took the

---

three served on the original committee that edited *The Journal.*" *PM,* 310.

21. "Benjamin Parvin (1727–?). Born and educated in Ireland, he was named for his grandfather, who had been imprisoned for his Quaker beliefs. After immigrating to America his father eventually settled in Berks County, PA, serving as county coroner, and later becoming a member of the Pennsylvania Assembly. Benjamin remained in Berks County, where he was surveyor and also served as coroner." *PM,* 310.

advantage of their weakness. Of this their chiefs have often complained at their treaties with the English.

Where cunning people pass counterfeits and impose that on others which is only good for nothing, it is considered as a wickedness, but to sell that to people which we know does them harm and which often works their ruin, for the sake of gain, manifests a hardened and corrupt heart and is an evil which demands the care of all true lovers of virtue to suppress. And while my mind this evening was thus employed, I also remembered that the people on the frontier, among whom this evil is too common, are often poor people, who venture to the outside of a colony that they may live more independent on such who are wealthy, who often set high rents on their land, being renewedly confirmed in a belief that if all our inhabitants lived according to sound wisdom, labouring to promote universal love and righteousness, and ceased from every inordinate desire after wealth and from all customs which are tinctured with luxury, the way would be easy for our inhabitants, though much more numerous than at present, to live comfortably on honest employments, without having that temptation they are often under of being drawn into schemes to make settlements on lands which have not been purchased of the Indians, or of applying to that wicked practice of selling rum to them.

10th day, 6th month. Set out early in the morning and crossed the western branch of Delaware, called the Great Lehigh, near Fort Allen; the water being high we went over in a canoe. Here we met an Indian and had some friendly conversation with him and gave him some biscuit, and he, having killed a deer, gave the Indians with us some of it. Then after travelling some miles we met several Indian men and women with a cow and horse and some household goods, who were lately come from their dwelling at Wyoming and going to settle at another place. We made them some small presents, and some of them understanding English, I told them my motive in coming into their country, with which they appeared satisfied. And one of our guides talking awhile with an ancient woman concerning us, the poor old woman came to my companion and me and took her leave of us with an appearance of sincere affection. So going on we pitched our tent near the banks of the same river, having laboured hard in crossing some of those mountains called the Blue Ridge. And by the roughness of the stones and the cavities between them and the steepness of the hills, it appeared dangerous, but we were preserved in safety, through the kindness of him whose works in those mountainous deserts appeared awful, toward whom my heart was turned during this day's travel.

Near our tent, on the sides of large trees peeled for that purpose were various representations of men going to and returning from the wars, and of some killed in battle, this being a path heretofore used by warriors. And as I walked about viewing those Indian histories, which were painted mostly in red but some with black, and thinking on the innumerable afflictions which the proud, fierce spirit produceth in the world—thinking on the toils and fatigues of warriors travelling over mountains and deserts, thinking on their miseries and distresses when wounded far from home by their enemies, and of their bruises and great weariness in chasing one another over the rocks and mountains, and of their restless, unquiet state of mind who live in this spirit, and of the hatred which mutually grows up in the minds of the children of those nations engaged in war with each other—during these meditations the desire to cherish the spirit of love and peace amongst these people arose in me.

This was the first night that we lodged in the woods, and being wet with travelling in the rain, the ground and our tent wet, and the bushes wet which we purposed [to] lay under our blankets, all looked discouraging. But I believed that it was the Lord who had thus far brought me forward and that he would dispose of me as he saw good, and therein I felt easy. So we kindled a fire with our tent door open to it; and with some bushes next the ground, and then our blankets, we made our bed, and lying down got some sleep. And in the morning feeling a little unwell, I went into the river all over. The water was cold, and soon after I felt fresh and well.

11th day, 6th month. The bushes being wet we tarried in our tent till about eight o'clock, then going on crossed a high mountain supposed to be upward of four miles wide, and the steepness on the north side exceeded all the others. We also crossed two swamps, and it raining near night, we pitched our tent and lodged.

About noon on our way we were overtaken by one of the Moravian brethren going to Wyalusing, and an Indian man with him who could talk English; and we, being together while our horses eat grass, had some friendly conversation; then they, travelling faster than we, soon left us.[22] This Moravian, I understood, had spent some time this spring at Wyalusing and was by some of them invited to come again.

12th day, 6th month, and first of the week. It being a rainy day we continued in our tent, and here I was led to think on the nature of the exercise which hath attended me. Love was the first motion, and then a concern arose to spend some time with the Indians, that I might feel and understand their life and the spirit they live in, if haply I might receive some instruction from them, or they be in any degree helped forward by my following the leadings of Truth amongst them. And as it pleased the Lord to make way for my going at a time when the troubles of war were increasing, and when by reason of much wet weather travelling was more difficult than usual at that season, I looked upon it as a more favourable opportunity to season my mind and bring me into a nearer sympathy with them. And as mine eye was to the great Father of Mercies, humbly desiring to learn what his will was concerning me, I was made quiet and content.

Our pilot's horse, though hoppled,[23] went away in the night, and after finding our own and searching some time for him, his footsteps were discovered in the path going back again, whereupon my kind companion went off in the rain, and after about seven hours returned with him, and here we lodged again, tying up our horses before we went to bed and loosing them to feed about break of day.

13th day, 6th month. The sun appearing, we set forward, and as I rode over the barren hills my meditations were on the alterations of the circumstances of the natives of this land since the coming in of the English. The lands

---

22. "The Moravian was David Zeisberger (1721–1808), the well-known missionary who spent most of his adult years, despite great hazards, ministering to the Indians of the Pennsylvania wilderness. The Moravians trace their origin to the evangelical movement in Bohemia led by John Huss, who suffered martyrdom in 1415. The sect grew rapidly in Bohemia and Moravia, and was severely persecuted. In 1722, Moravian refugees settled on the estate of Count Zinzendorf in the town of Herrnhut in Saxony. In 1727 a communal religious experience by members of the group inspired them to several evangelistic efforts, of which the mission to the American Indians was one." *PM,* 127, note 16.

23. Hoppled. Woolman's term for the more widely used "hobbled."

near the sea are conveniently situated for fishing. The lands near the rivers, where the tides flow, and some above, are in many places fertile and not mountainous, while the running of the tides makes passing up and down easy with any kind of traffic. Those natives have in some places, for trifling considerations, sold their inheritance so favourably situated, and in other places been driven back by superior force, so that in many places, as their way of clothing themselves is now altered from what it was and they far remote from us, [they] have to pass over mountains, swamps, and barren deserts, where travelling is very troublesome, in bringing their skins and furs to trade with us.

By the extending of English settlements and partly by English hunters, those wild beasts they chiefly depend on for a subsistence are not so plenty as they were, and people too often, for the sake of gain, open a door for them to waste their skins and furs in purchasing a liquor which tends to the ruin of them and their families.

My own will and desires being now very much broken and my heart with much earnestness turned to the Lord, to whom alone I looked for help in the dangers before me, I had a prospect of the English along the coast for upward of nine hundred miles where I have travelled. And the favourable situation of the English and the difficulties attending the natives in many places, and the Negroes, were open before me. And a weighty, and heavenly care came over my mind, and love filled my heart toward all mankind, in which I felt a strong engagement that we might be obedient to the Lord while in tender mercies he is yet calling to us, and so attend to pure universal righteousness as to give no just cause of offense to the Gentiles, who do not profess Christianity, whether the blacks from Africa or the native inhabitants of this continent. And here I was led into a close, laborious inquiry whether I, as an individual, kept clear from all things which tended to stir up or were connected with wars, either in this land or Africa, and my heart was deeply concerned that in future I might in all things keep steadily to the pure Truth and live and walk in the plainness and simplicity of a sincere follower of Christ.

And in this lonely journey I did this day greatly bewail the spreading of a wrong spirit, believing that the prosperous, convenient situation of the English requires a constant attention to divine love and wisdom, to guide and support us in a way answerable to the will of that good, gracious, and almighty Being who hath an equal regard to all mankind. And here luxury and covetousness, with the numerous oppressions and other evils attending them, appeared very afflicting to me, and I felt in that which is immutable that the seeds of great calamity and desolation are sown and growing fast on this continent. Nor have I words sufficient to set forth that longing I then felt that we who are placed along coast; and have tasted the love and goodness of God, might arise in his strength and like faithful messengers labour to check the growth of these seeds, that they may not ripen to the ruin of our posterity.

We reached the Indian settlement at Wyoming, and here we were told that an Indian runner had been at that place a day or two before us and brought news of the Indians taking an English fort westward and destroying the people, and that they were endeavouring to take another—and also that another Indian runner came there about midnight the night next before we got there, who came from a town about ten miles above Wyalusing and brought news that some Indian warriors from distant parts came to that town with two English scalps and told the people that it was war with the English.

Our pilots took us to the house of a very ancient man, and soon after we had put in our baggage, there came a man from another Indian house some distance off. And I, perceiving there was a man near the door, went out; and he having a tomahawk wrapped under his match-coat out of sight, as I approached him he took it in his hand. I, however, went forward, and speaking to him in a friendly way perceived he understood some English. My companion then coming out, we had some talk with him concerning the nature of our visit in these parts; and then he, going into the house with us and talking with our pilots, soon appeared friendly and sat down and smoked his pipe. Though his taking his hatchet in his hand at the instant I drew near him had a disagreeable appearance, I believe he had no other intent than to be in readiness in case any violence was offered to him.

Hearing the news brought by these Indian runners, and being told by the Indians where we lodged that what Indians were about Wyoming expected in a few days to move to some larger towns, I thought that to all outward appearance it was dangerous travelling at this time, and was after a hard day's journey brought into a painful exercise at night, in which I had to trace back and feel over the steps I had taken from my first moving in the visit. And though I had to bewail some weakness which at times had attended me, yet I could not find that I had ever given way to wilful disobedience. And then as I believed I had under a sense of duty come thus far, I was now earnest in spirit beseeching the Lord to show me what I ought to do.

In this great distress I grew jealous of myself,[24] lest the desire of reputation as a man firmly settled to persevere through dangers, or the fear of disgrace arising on my returning without performing the visit, might have some place in me. Thus I lay full of thoughts great part of the night, while my beloved companion lay and slept by me, till the Lord my gracious Father, who saw the conflicts of my soul, was pleased to give quietness. Then was I again strengthened to commit my life and all things relating thereto into his heavenly hands; and getting a little sleep toward day, when morning came we arose.

And then on the 14th day, 6th month, we sought out and visited all the Indians hereabouts that we could meet with, they being chiefly in one place about a mile from where we lodged, in all perhaps twenty. Here I expressed the care I had on my mind for their good and told them that true love had made me willing thus to leave my family to come and see the Indians and speak with them in their houses. Some of them appeared kind and friendly. So we took our leave of these Indians and went up the river Susquehanna about three miles to the house of an Indian called Jacob January, who had killed his hog, and the women were making store of bread and preparing to move up the river. Here our pilots left their canoe when they came down in the spring, which lying dry was leaky, so that we, being detained some hours, had a good deal of friendly conversation with the family; and eating dinner with them we made them some small presents. Then putting our baggage in the canoe, some of them pushed slowly up the stream, and the rest of us rode our horses; and swimming them over a creek called Lahawahamunk we pitched our tent a little about it, there being a shower in the evening. And in a sense of God's goodness in helping me in my distress, sustaining me

---

24. "Jealous of myself" implies that Woolman meant "fearful of self," i.e., that he would listen to the self rather than the leadings of the spirit within.

under trials, and inclining my heart to trust in him, I lay down in a humble, bowed frame of mind and had a comfortable night's lodging.

15th day, 6th month. Proceeded forward till afternoon, when, a storm appearing, we met our canoe at an appointed place; and the rain continuing, we stayed all night, which was so heavy that it beat through our tent and wet us and our baggage. 16th day. We found on our way abundance of trees blown down with the storm yesterday and had occasion reverently to consider the kind dealings of the Lord, who provided a safe place for us in a valley while this storm continued. By the falling of abundance of trees across our path we were much hindered, and in some swamps our way was so stopped that we got through with extreme difficulty.

I had this day often to consider myself as a sojourner in this world, and a belief in the all-sufficiency of God to support his people in their pilgrimage felt comfortable to me, and I was industriously employed to get to a state of perfect resignation.

We seldom saw our canoe but at appointed places, by reason of the path going off from the river; and this afternoon Job Chilaway,[25] an Indian from Wyalusing, who talks good English and is acquainted with several people in and about Philadelphia, he met our people on the river, and understanding where we expected to lodge, pushed back about six miles and came to us after night. And in a while our own canoe came, it being hard work pushing up stream. Job told us that an Indian came in haste to their town yesterday and told them that three warriors, coming from some distance, lodged in a town above Wyalusing a few nights past and that these three men were going against the English at Juniata. Job was going down the river to the province store at Shamokin. Though I was so far favoured with health as to continue travelling, yet through the various difficulties in our journey and the different way of living from what I had been used to, I grew weak. And the news of these warriors being on their march so near us, and not

---

25. "Job Chilaway (?-1796). An Indian with a fluent command of English, he frequently served as a guide and interpreter for government and army officials. He was a convert to the Moravian church and a friend of Papunehang at Wyalusing. He played a prominent role in complicated negotiations over land involving the Indians, the government, and the Bethlehem Synod of the Moravian church." *PM,* 307–8; see note 26, below.

knowing whether we might not fall in with them, it was a fresh trial of my faith; and though through the strength of divine love I had several times been enabled to commit myself to the divine disposal, I still found the want of my strength to be renewed, that I might persevere therein. And my cries for help were put up to the Lord, who in great mercy gave me a resigned heart, in which I found quietness.

17th day, 6th month. Parting from Job Chilaway, we went on and reached Wyalusing about the middle of the afternoon, and the first Indian that we saw was a woman of a modest countenance, with a babe, who first spake to our pilot and then with a harmonious voice expressed her gladness at seeing us, having before heard of our coming. Then by the direction of our pilot we sat down on a log, and he went to the town to tell the people that we were come. My companion and I sitting thus together in a deep inward stillness, the poor woman came and sat near us; and great awfulness coming over us, we rejoiced in a sense of God's love manifested to our poor souls.

After a while we heard a conch shell blow several times, and then came John Curtis and another Indian man who kindly invited us into a house near the town, where we found I suppose about sixty people sitting in silence. And after sitting a short time, I stood up and in some tenderness of spirit acquainted them with the nature of my visit and that a concern for their good had made me willing to come thus far to see them—all in a few short sentences, which some of them, understanding, interpreted to the others; and there appeared gladness amongst them. Then I showed them my certificate, which was explained to them; and the Moravian who overtook us on the way, being now here, bid me welcome.

18th day, 6th month. We rested ourselves this forenoon, and the Indians, knowing that the Moravian and I were of different religious Societies, and as some of their people had encouraged him to come and stay awhile with them, were, I believe, concerned that no jarring or discord might be in their meetings; and they, I suppose having conferred together, acquainted me that the people at my request would at any time come together and hold meetings, and also told me that they expected the Moravian would speak in their settled meetings, which are commonly held morning and near evening. So I found liberty in my heart to speak to the Moravian and told him of the care I felt on my mind for the good of these people, and that I believed no ill effects would follow it if I sometimes spake in their meetings when love engaged me thereto, without calling them together at times when they did not meet of course; whereupon he expressed his good will toward my speaking at any time all that I found in my heart to say.

So near evening I was at their meeting, where the pure gospel love was felt, to the tendering some of our hearts. And the interpreters, endeavoring to acquaint the people with what I said, in short sentences, found some difficulty, as none of them were quite perfect in the English and Delaware tongue. So they helped one another and we laboured along, divine love attending. And afterwards feeling my mind covered with the spirit of prayer, I told the interpreters that I found it in my heart to pray to God and believed if I prayed right he would hear me, and expressed my willingness for them to omit interpreting; so our meeting ended with a degree of divine love. And before the people went out I observed Papunehang[26] (the man who had been zealous in labouring for a reformation in that town, being then very tender) spoke to one of the interpreters, and I was afterward told that he said in substance as follows: "I love to feel where words come from."

19th day, 6th month, and first of the week. This morning in the meeting the Indian who came with the Moravian, being also a member of that Society, prayed, and then the Moravian spake a short time to the people. And in the afternoon, they coming together and my heart being filled with a heavenly care for their good, I spake to them awhile by interpreters, but none of them being perfect in the work. And I feeling the current of love run strong, told the interpreters that I believed some of the people would understand

---

26. "Papunehang (ca. 1705–1775). A chief of the Delaware Indians, he was a spiritual leader of his people both before and after becoming a Christian. He was converted by David Zeisberger. He represented his tribe in meetings with other tribes, colonial officials, and with the Quakers. His gentle disposition and spiritual sensitivity greatly impressed the white Christians who knew him." *PM,* 309–10. Tragically, Papunehang's tribe may be the same Indians who after becoming Christian moved or were moved to Gnadenhutten, Ohio to escape persecution but there the entire tribe, except for a couple of teenagers, were massacred by the whites in 1782. Woolman was among the delegation that met with the Native Americans in their visit in 1760 to Philadelphia. Compare Woolman's and the other account of that meeting in this book.

me, and so proceeded, in which exercise I believe the Holy Ghost wrought on some hearts to edification, where all the words were not understood. I looked upon it as a time of divine favour, and my heart was tendered and truly thankful before the Lord. And after I sat down one of the interpreters seemed spirited up to give the Indians the substance of what I said.

Before our first meeting this morning, I was led to meditate on the manifold difficulties of these Indians, who by the permission of the Six Nations dwell in these parts, and a near sympathy with them was raised in me; and my heart being enlarged in the love of Christ, I thought that the affectionate care of a good man for his only brother in affliction does not exceed what I then felt for that people.

I came to this place through much trouble, and though through the mercies of God I believed that if I died in the journey it would be well with me, yet the thoughts of falling into the hands of Indian warriors was in times of weakness afflicting to me; and being of a tender constitution of body, the thoughts of captivity amongst them was at times grievous, as supposing that they, being strong and hardy, might demand service of me beyond what I could well bear. But the Lord alone was my helper, and I believed if I went into captivity it would be for some good end. And thus from time to time my mind was centered in resignation, in which I always found quietness. And now this day, though I had the same dangerous wilderness between me and home, I was inwardly joyful that the Lord had strengthened me to come on this visit and manifested a fatherly care over me in my poor lowly condition, when in mine own eyes I appeared inferior to many amongst the Indians.

When the last-mentioned meeting was ended, it being night, Papunehang went to bed; and one of the interpreters sitting by me, I observed Papunehang spoke with a harmonious voice, I suppose a minute or two, and asking the interpreter, was told that he was expressing his thankfulness to God for the favours he had received that day, and prayed that he would continue to favour him with that same which he had experienced in that meeting—that though Papunehang had before agreed to receive the Moravian and join with them, he still appeared kind and loving to us.

20th day, 6th month. Was at two meetings and silent in them. 21st day. This morning in meeting my heart was enlarged in pure love amongst them, and in short plain sentences expressed several things that rested upon me, which one of the interpreters gave the people pretty readily, after which the meeting ended in supplication. And I had cause humbly to acknowledge the loving-kindness of the Lord toward us, and then I believed that a door remained open for the faithful disciples of Jesus Christ to labour amongst these people.

I now, feeling my mind at liberty to return, took my leave of them in general at the conclusion of what I said in meeting, and so we prepared to go homeward. But some of their most active men told us that when we were ready to move, the people would choose to come and shake hands with us, which those who usually came to meeting did. And from a secret draught in my mind, I went amongst some who did not use to go to meeting and took my leave of them also. And the Moravian and his Indian interpreter appeared respectful to us at parting. This town stands on the bank of Susquehanna and consists, I believe, of about forty houses, mostly compact together: some about thirty foot long and eighteen wide (some bigger, some less), mostly built of split plank, one end set in the ground and the other pinned to a plate, and then rafters and covered with bark. I understand a great flood last winter overflowed the chief part of the ground where the town stands, and some were now about moving their houses to higher ground.

We expected only two Indians to be our company, but when we were ready to go, we found many of them were going to Bethlehem with skins and furs, who chose to go in company with us. So they loaded two canoes which they desired us to go in, telling us that the waters were so raised with the rains that the horses should be taken by such who were better acquainted with the fording places. So we, with several Indians, went in the canoes, and others went on horses, there being seven besides ours. And we meeting with the horseman once on the way by appointment, and then near night a little below a branch called Tunkhannock, we lodged there; and some of the young men, going out a little before dusk with their guns, brought in a deer.

22nd day, 6th month. Through diligence we reached Wyoming before night and understood the Indians were mostly gone from this place. Here we went up a small creek into the woods with our canoes and, pitching our tent, carried out our baggage; and before dark our horses came to us.

23rd day, 6th month. In the morning their horses were loaded, and we prepared our baggage and so set forward, being in all fourteen, and with diligent travelling were favoured to get near half way to Fort Allen. The land on this road from Wyoming to our frontier being mostly poor, and good grass scarce, they chose a piece of low ground to lodge on, as the best for grazing. And I, having sweat much in travelling and being weary, slept sound. I perceived in the night that I had taken cold, of which I was favoured to get better soon.

24th day, 6th month. We passed Fort Allen and lodged near it in the woods, having forded the westerly branch of Delaware three times, and thereby had a shorter way and missed going over the top of the Blue Mountains, called the Second Ridge. In the second time, fording where the river cuts through the mountain, the waters being rapid and pretty deep and my companion's mare being a tall, tractable animal, he sundry times drove her back through the river, and they loaded her with the burdens of some small horses which they thought not sufficient to come through with their loads. The troubles westward, and the difficulty for Indians to pass through our frontier, I apprehend was one reason why so many came, as expecting that our being in company would prevent the outside inhabitants from being surprised.

25th day, 6th month. We reached Bethlehem, taking care on the way to keep foremost and to acquaint people on and near the road who these Indians were. This we found very needful, for that the frontier inhabitants were often alarmed at the report of English being killed by Indians westward.

Amongst our company were some who I did not remember to have seen at meeting, and some of these at first were very reserved, but we being several days together and behaving friendly toward them and making them suitable returns for the services they did us, they became more free and sociable.

26th day, 6th month, and first of the week. Having carefully endeavoured to settle all affairs with the Indians relative to our journey, we took leave of them, and I thought they generally parted with us affectionately. So we, getting to Richland, had a very comfortable meeting amongst our friends. Here I parted with my kind friend and companion Benjamin Parvin, and accompanied by my friend Samuel Foulke we rode to John Cadwalader's, from whence I reached home the next day, where I found my family middling well. And they and my friends all along appeared glad to see me return from a journey which they apprehended dangerous. But my mind while I was out had been so employed in striving for a perfect resignation, and I had so often been confirmed in a belief that whatever the Lord might be pleased to allot for me would work for good, [that] I was careful lest I should admit any degree of selfishness in being glad overmuch, and laboured to improve by those trials in such a manner as my gracious Father and Protector intends for me.

Between the English inhabitants and Wyalusing we had only a narrow path, which in many places is much grown up with bushes and interrupted by abundance of trees lying across it, which together with the mountains, swamps, and rough stones, it is a difficult road to travel, and the more so for that rattlesnakes abound there, of which we killed four—that people who have never been in such places have but an imperfect idea of them. But I was not only taught patience but also made thankful to God, who thus led me about and instructed me that I might have a quick and lively feeling of the afflictions of my fellow creatures whose situation in life is difficult.

from Chapter 10
1769–1770

...after a few weeks it pleased the Lord to visit me with a pleurisy, and after I had lain a few days and felt the disorder very grievous, I was thoughtful how it might end.[27] I had of late through various exercises been much weaned from the pleasant things of this life, and I now thought if it was the Lord's will to put an end to my labours and graciously receive me into the arms of his mercy, death would be acceptable to me; but if it was his will to further refine me under affliction and make me in any degree useful in his church, I desired not to die. I may with thankfulness say that in this case I felt resignedness wrought in me and had no inclination to send for a doctor, believing if it was the Lord's will through outward means to raise me up, some sympathizing friends would be sent to minister to me, which

---

27. This passage describes the illness in which Woolman had the vision described, two years later, in chapter 12, pages 52-54, below.

were accordingly. But though I was carefully attended, yet the disorder was at times so heavy that I had no thoughts of recovery.

One night in particular my bodily distress was great: my feet grew cold, and cold increased up my legs toward my body, and at that time I had no inclination to ask my nurse to apply anything warm to my feet, expecting my end was near. And after I had lain, I believe, near ten hours in this condition, I closed my eyes, thinking whether I might now be delivered out of the body; but in these awful moments my mind was livingly opened to behold the church, and strong engagements were begotten in me for the everlasting well-being of my fellow creatures. And I felt in the spring of pure love that I might remain some time longer in the body, in filling up according to my measure that which remains of the afflictions of Christ and in labouring for the good of the church, after which I requested my nurse to apply warmth to my feet, and I revived. And the next night, feeling a weighty exercise of spirit and having a solid Friend sitting up with me, I requested him to write what I said, which he did as follows:

> 4th day, 1st month, 1770, about five in the morning. I have seen in the light of the Lord that the day is approaching when the man that is the most wise in human policies shall be the greatest fool, and the arm that is mighty to support injustice shall be broken to pieces. The enemies of righteousness shall make a terrible rattle and shall mightily torment one another. For he that is omnipotent is rising up to judgment and will plead the cause of the oppressed. And he commanded me to open the vision.

Near a week after this, feeling my mind livingly opened, I sent for a neighbour, who at my request wrote as follows:

> The place of prayer is a precious habitation, for I now saw that the prayers of the saints was precious incense. And a trumpet was given me that I might sound forth this language, that the children might hear it and be invited to gather to this precious habitation, where the prayers of

saints, as precious incense, ariseth up before the throne of God and the Lamb. I saw this habitation to be safe, to be inwardly quiet, when there was great stirrings and commotions in the world.

Prayer at this day in pure resignation is a precious place. The trumpet is sounded; the call goes forth to the church that she gather to the place of pure inward prayer, and her habitation is safe....

from Chapter 12
1772

8th day, 6th month, 1772. Landed at London and went straightway to the Yearly Meeting of Ministers and Elders which had been gathered about (I suppose) half an hour. In this meeting my mind was humbly contrite. Afternoon meeting of business opened, which by adjournments held near a week. In these meetings I often felt a living concern for the establishment of Friends in the pure life of Truth, and my heart was enlarged in the meeting of ministers, meeting of business, and in several meetings for public worship, and I felt my mind united in true love to the faithful labourers now gathered from the several parts of this Yearly Meeting.

15th, 6th month. Left London and went to Quarterly Meeting at Hertford.

1st day, 7th month, 1772. Have been at Quarterly Meetings at Sherrington, at Northampton, at Banbury, at Shipston, and had sundry meetings between. My mind hath been bowed under a sense of divine goodness manifested amongst us. My heart hath often been enlarged in true love amongst ministers and elders and in public meetings, that through the Lord's goodness I believe it hath been a fresh visitation to many, in particular to the youth....

16th, 8th month, and first of week. Was at Settle. It hath of late been a time of inward poverty, under which my mind hath been preserved in a watchful, tender state, feeling for the mind of the Holy Leader, and find peace in the labours I have passed through.

On inquiry in many places I find the price of rye about 5 shillings; wheat about 8 shillings; oatmeal 12 shillings for 120 pound; mutton from 3 pence to 5 pence per pound; bacon from 7 pence to 9 pence; cheese from 4 pence to 6 pence; butter from 8 pence to 10 pence; house rent for a poor man from 25 shillings to 40 shillings per year, to be paid weekly; wood for fire very scarce and dear; coal in some places 2 shillings 6 pence per hundredweight, but near the pits not a quarter so much. Oh, may the wealthy consider the poor!

The wages of labouring men in several counties toward London, 10 pence per day in common business; the employer finds small beer and the labourer finds his own food; but in harvest and hay time, wages about 1 shilling and the labourer have all his diet. In some parts of the north of England poor labouring men have their food where they work and appear in common to do rather better than nearer London. Industrious women who spin in the factories get some 4 pence, some 5 pence, and so on: 6, 7, 8, 9 pence, or 10 pence, and find their own house-room and diet. Great numbers of poor people live chiefly on bread and water in the southern parts of England and some in the northern parts, and many poor children learn not to read. May those who have plenty lay these things to heart!

Stagecoaches frequently go upwards of a hundred miles in 24 hours, and I have heard Friends say in several places that it is common for horses to be killed with hard driving, and many others driven till they grow blind. These coaches running chief part of the night do often run over foot people in the dark.

Postboys pursue their business, each one to his stage, all night through the winter. Some boys who ride long stages suffer greatly in winter nights, and at several places I have heard of their being froze to death. So great is the hurry in the spirit of this world that in aiming to do business quick and to gain wealth the creation at this day doth loudly groan!

As my journey hath been without a horse, I have had several offers of being assisted on my way in these stages, but have not been in them, nor have I had freedom to send letters by these posts in the present way of their riding, the stages being so fixed and one boy dependent on another as to time, that they commonly go upward of 100 mile in 24 hours, and in the cold long winter nights the poor boys suffer much.

I heard in America of the way of these posts and cautioned Friends in the General Meeting of Ministers and Elders at Philadelphia and in the Yearly

Meeting of Ministers and Elders at London not to send letters to me on any common occasion by post. And though on this account I may be likely to hear seldomer from the family I left behind, yet for righteousness sake I am through divine favour made content.

I have felt great distress of mind since I came on this island, on account of the members of our Society being mixed with the world in various sorts of business and traffic carried on in impure channels. Great is the trade to Africa for slaves! And in loading these ships abundance of people are employed in the factories, amongst whom are many of our Society! Friends in early times refused on a religious principle to make or trade in superfluities, of which we have many large testimonies on record, but for want of faithfulness some gave way, even some whose examples were of note in Society, and from thence others took more liberty. Members of our Society worked in superfluities and bought and sold them, and thus dimness of sight came over many. At length Friends got into the use of some superfluities in dress and in the furniture of their houses, and this hath spread from less to more, till superfluity of some kinds is common amongst us.

In this declining state many look at the example one of another and too much neglect the pure feeling of Truth. Of late years a deep exercise hath attended my mind that Friends may dig deep, may carefully cast forth the loose matter and get down to the rock, the sure foundation, and there hearken to that divine voice which gives a clear and certain sound; and I have felt in that which doth not deceive that if Friends who have known the Truth keep in that tenderness of heart where all views of outward gain are given up, and their trust is only on the Lord, he will graciously lead some to be patterns of deep self-denial in things relating to trade and handicraft labour, and that some who have plenty of the treasures of this world will example in a plain frugal life and pay wages to such whom they may hire, more liberally than is now customary in some places.

23rd, 8th month. Was this day at Preston Patrick. Here I dreamed of mother. Had a comfortable meeting. I have several times been entertained at the houses of Friends who had sundry things about them which had the appearance of outward greatness, and as I have kept inward, way hath opened for conversation in private, in which divine goodness hath favoured us together with heart-tendering times.

A deviation amongst us as a Society from that simplicity that there is in Christ becoming so general, and the trade from this island to Africa for slaves, and other trades carried on through oppressive channels, and abundance of the inhabitants being employed in factories to support a trade in which there is unrighteousness, and some growing outwardly great by gain of this sort: the weight of this degeneracy hath lain so heavy upon me, the depth of this revolt been so evident, and desires in my heart been so ardent for a reformation, so ardent that we might come to that right use of things where, living on a little, we might inhabit that holy mountain on which they neither hurt nor destroy! and may not only stand clear from oppressing our fellow creatures, but may be so disentangled from connections in interest with known oppressors, that in us may be fulfilled that prophecy: "Thou shalt be far from oppression" [Is. 54:14]. Under the weight of this exercise the sight of innocent birds in the branches and sheep in the pastures, who act according to the will of their Creator, hath at times tended to mitigate my trouble.

26th day, 8th month, 1772. Being now at George Crosfield's, in Westmoreland County in England, I feel a concern to commit to writing that which to me hath been a case uncommon. In a time of sickness with the pleurisy a little upward of two years and a half ago, I was brought so near the gates of death that I forgot my name. Being then desirous to know who I was, I saw a mass of matter of a dull gloomy colour, between the south and the east, and was informed that this mass was human beings in as great misery as they could be and live, and that I was mixed in with them and henceforth might not consider myself as a distinct or separate being. In this state I remained several hours. I then heard a soft, melodious voice, more pure and harmonious than any voice I had heard with my ears before, and I believed it was the voice of an angel who spake to other angels. The words were, *"John Woolman is dead."* I soon remembered that I once was John Woolman, and being assured that I was alive in the body, I greatly wondered what that heavenly voice could mean. I believed beyond doubting that it was the voice of an holy angel, but as yet it was a mystery to me.

I was then carried in spirit to the mines, where poor oppressed people were digging rich treasures for those called Christians, and heard them blaspheme the name of Christ, at which I was grieved, for his name to me was precious. Then I was informed that these heathens were told that those who oppressed them were the followers of Christ, and they said amongst themselves: "If Christ directed them to use us in this sort, then Christ is a cruel tyrant."

All this time the song of the angel remained a mystery, and in the morning my dear wife and some others coming to my bedside, I asked them if they knew who I was; and they, telling me I was John Woolman, thought I was only light-headed, for I told them not what the angel said, nor was I disposed to talk much to anyone, but was very desirous to get so deep that I might understand this mystery.

My tongue was often so dry that I could not speak till I had moved it about and gathered some moisture, and as I lay still for a time, at length I felt divine power prepare my mouth that I could speak, and then I said: "I am crucified with Christ, nevertheless I live; yet not I, but Christ that liveth in me, and the life I now live in the flesh is by faith in the Son of God, who loved me and gave himself for me" [Gal. 2:20]. Then the mystery was opened, and I perceived there was joy in heaven over a sinner who had repented and that that language *John Woolman is dead* meant no more that the death of my own will.

Soon after this I coughed and raised much bloody matter, which I had not during this vision, and now my natural understanding returned as before. Here I saw that people getting silver vessels to set off their tables at entertainments was often stained with worldly glory, and that in the present state of things, I should take heed how I fed myself from out of silver vessels.

Soon after my recovery I, going to our Monthly Meeting, dined at a Friend's house, where drink was brought in silver vessels and not in any other. And I, wanting some drink, told him my case with weeping, and he ordered some drink for me in another vessel.

The like I went through in several Friends' houses in America and have also in England since I came here, and have cause with humble reverence to acknowledge the loving-kindness of my Heavenly Father, who hath preserved me in such a tender frame of mind that none, I believe, have ever been offended at what I have said on that occasion. John Woolman.[28]

---

28. "The signature 'John Woolman' has been crossed out [in the manuscript], probably by the original editorial committee." *PM*, 187.

After this sickness I spake not in public meetings for worship for near one year, but my mind was very often in company with the oppressed slaves as I sat in meetings, and though under this dispensation I was shut up from speaking, yet the spring of the gospel ministry was many times livingly opened in me and the divine gift operated by abundance of weeping in feeling the oppression of this people.

It being now so long since I passed through this dispensation and the matter remaining fresh and livingly on my mind, I believe it safest for me to write it....

Having of late travelled often in wet weather through narrow streets in towns and villages, where dirtiness under foot and the scent arising from that filth which more or less infects the air of all thick settled towns, and I, being but weakly, have felt distress both in body and mind with that which is impure. In these journeys I have been where much cloth hath been dyed and sundry times walked over ground where much of their dye-stuffs have drained away.

Here I have felt a longing in my mind that people might come into cleanness of spirit, cleanness of person, cleanness about their houses and garments. Some who are great carry delicacy to a great height themselves, and yet the real cleanliness is not generally promoted. Dyes being invented partly to please the eye and partly to hide dirt, I have felt in this weak state, travelling in dirtiness and affected with unwholesome scents, a strong desire that the nature of dyeing cloth to hide dirt may be more fully considered.

To hide dirt in our garments appears opposite to real cleanliness. To wash garments and keep them sweet, this appears cleanly. Through giving way to hiding dirt in our garments, a spirit which would cover that which is disagreeable is strengthened. Real cleanness becometh a holy people, but hiding that which is not clean by colouring our garments appears contrary to the sweetness of sincerity.

Through some sorts of dyes cloth is less useful. And if the value of dye-stuffs, the expense of dyeing, and the damage done to cloth were all added together and that expense applied to keep all sweet and clean, how much more cleanly would people be.

Near large towns there are many beasts slain to supply the market, and from their blood, etc., ariseth that which mixeth in the air. This, with the cleaning of many stables and other scents, the air in cities in a calm, wet-tish time is so opposite to the clear pure country air that I believe even the minds of people are in some degree hindered from the pure operation of the Holy Spirit, where they breathe a great deal in it. With God all things are possible, and the sincere in heart find help under the greatest difficulties, but I believe if Truth be singly attended to, way may open for some to live a country life who now are in cities.

Copy of a Letter

York, 22nd day, 9th month, 1772

Beloved Friend,[29]

When I followed the trade of a tailor, I had a feeling of that which pleased the proud mind in people, and growing uneasy, was strengthened to leave off that which was superfluous in my trade.

When I was at your house, I believe I had a sense of the pride of people being gratified in some part of the business thou followest and feel a concern in pure love to endeavour thus to inform thee of it.

Christ our leader is worthy of being followed in his leadings at all times. The enemy gets many on his side. Oh, that we may not be divided between the two, but may be wholly on the side of Christ.

In true love to you all I remain thy friend,

John Woolman

9th month, 28, '72.

Being now at the house of my friend Thomas Priestman in the city of York, so weak in body that I know not how my sickness may end, I am

---

29. "The 'Friend' was probably John Wilson, son of Rachel Wilson." *PM*, 191, note 20; "[Rachel Wilson and husband Isaac Wilson] had nine children. An eloquent Quaker preacher, she traversed the British Isles, where she was on friendly terms with George Whitefield. In 1768 and 1769 she travelled on horseback through the American colonies. At the Philadelphia Yearly Meeting of 1769, she interrupted her testimony to speak directly to Woolman, who was then undecided as to whether to visit the West Indies." *PM*, 312.

concerned to leave in writing a case the remembrance whereof hath often affected me. An honest hearted Friend in America, who departed this life a little less than a year ago, some months before his departure, he told me in substance as follows:

That he saw in a dream or night vision a great pond of blood from which a fog rose up. Some distance from him he saw this fog spread round about and great numbers of people walking backwards and forward in it, the garments of whom had a tincture of blood in 'em. I perceived he apprehended that by the pool of blood was represented the state of those hardhearted men through whose means much blood is shed in Africa and many lives destroyed through insupportable stench and other hardships in crossing the sea, and through extreme oppression bring many slaves to an untimely end, and that the fog in which the people were walking represented the gain arising on merchandise or traffic which many were taking hold of and, at the same time, knew that the gain was the gain of oppression.

This Friend, in his last sickness having several days had an inclination to see me, at length sent a messenger and I without delay went. He asked to be with me in private, which was granted; he then told me some matters in particular in regard to the gain of oppression, which he felt not easy to leave the world without opening to me. All this time he appeared calm and quiet, and the family coming in by his consent, death in about one hour appeared evidently upon him, and I believe in about five hours from my going in he quietly breathed his last; and as I believe he left no memorandum in writing of that dream or vision of the night, at this time I believe it seasonable for me to do it.[30]

John Woolman

---

30.   "The entry for September 28 appears to have been dictated by Woolman and written by someone else, probably Thomas Priestman.…The signature, in very shaky handwriting, appears to be Woolman's own." *PM,* 192, note 21; The Friend who told Woolman this dream has been identified as his brother Abner Woolman, who died in November 1771. Geoffrey Plank, *John Woolman's Path to the Peaceable Kingdom: A Quaker in the British Empire,* 217.

Selected Letters (1760–1772)

Woolman's letter to his wife Sarah Ellis Woolman,
31st, 7th month, 1772, from north of England

The letters in this section are selected from among Woolman's personal letters, as distinguished from the epistles directed to organized bodies of Friends, which he authored or co-authored. About fifty such letters have been preserved and more are still being discovered.

Those included here were selected with two considerations in mind: (1) they cast light on three major journeys which are treated in detail in The Journal, *the journey to the New England Yearly Meeting in 1760, to the Native Americans at Wyalusing in 1763, and to England in 1772,* and (2) they provide insight into Woolman's relations with members of his family and close friends. Of particular interest are Woolman's letters to his wife. Those who have read only The Journal *may get the impression that Woolman almost never wrote home while on his several extended trips. The examples which follow should correct that impression.*

In the letters, Woolman often expressed a personal, experiential dimension of his faith not so apparent in his other writings, and we see his careful use of language in expressing a systematic yet intuitive description of his "readings" of the inward spirit. For example, in Letter 16 from England, addressed to the children of Stephen Comfort, he writes, "I cannot form a concern, but when a concern cometh, I endeavor to be obedient." It is interesting to note, even in personal correspondence, Woolman never forgot his social and religious concerns.

The letters are arranged in chronological order, so far as the dates can be determined. All but those numbered 11 and 12 are based on Amelia Mott Gummere's The Journal and Essays of John Woolman, *with dates as they appear in the Gummere text. Readers should note that in these letters the day of the month generally comes first, following by month and year.*

Letters 1–5 have to do with Woolman's long journey to New England of 1760 described in Journal *chapter 7. His purpose was to visit the New England Yearly Meeting sessions in Newport, Rhode Island, and as his account shows, to bring his concerns about slavery to New England Friends. It is useful to read Mercy Redman's account of the same trip, in Related Writings by Contemporaries in this book.*

1.

18: 5: & first of week, 1760

Dearly beloved Wife,

My companion and I are now at Lynn in health about fifteen miles eastward from Boston.

I have wrote several letters to thee, expecting thou will be glad to hear that I am well, and I write the oftener for that I suppose they may not all come directly to thy hands.

It would be agreeable to me to hear from you, not having had any intelligence concerning you since I saw you, nor do I expect any soon as I am continually going from home. But should way open for our journey I hope to be at the further end of it in less than two weeks, and then return toward Newport Yearly Meeting.

I remember thee and my child often, with much nearness of affection, believing thou art somewhat lonesome in my absence, and the most comfortable thoughts I have on the subjects are that a good and gracious GOD governs the universe, who makes all things work for good to them that love him, of which number I trust thou art one. My love to my dear friends about home.

John Woolman

2.

Newport 14 6 1760

Dear wife,

I have heard not from home after I left you till two days ago I received thy two letters, one sent by B.A. and other by H.F. which were truly acceptable to me.[31]

I hear by William Lightfoot thou hast been poorly, but at the time of his passing by was better. Thy not mentioning it in thy letters, I consider as an intended kindness to me by forbearing to contribute to the increase of my exercise. I feel a most tender concern for thee as knowing thy condition

---

31.   H.F. is Hannah Foster. B.A. remains unidentified. *AMG*, 61, note 3, see also pp. 538–39.

to be attended with difficulty, and find at times a disposition to hasten for thy sake. But such is the weight of the work I am engaged in, and such the baptisms with which I have been baptized, that I see a necessity for all nature to stand silent. I know not that I ever have had a sharper conflict in spirit, or better understood what it was to take up the cross, than of late, the depth of which exercise is known only to the Almighty; and yet my beloved companion Samuel hath been a true and faithful sympathizer with me. I am humbly thankful to my gracious Father, who has brought my mind in a good degree to be resigned to him.

From him my being is derived. My life from one minute to another is sustained by him. All I have are his gifts, and I am endeavouring (though in weakness) to surrender all to him. My care about thee and my child is much greater than any other care (as to the things of this life) but my comfort hath all along been that a greater than I is careful for you, to whose gracious protection I recommend you.

The friends from our parts are all here and appear to be well. We have been generally pretty well, have got forward on our journey. There remains about 14 meetings besides Nantucket which we have not been at. Should we be favoured to get through them we expect to go for Oblong in York Government.

Spare no cost to make thy life comfortable as may be. I say so because I heard by H.F thou hast been disappointed about a young woman.[32]

My love is to all my dear friends.

John Woolman

3.
Newport 17 6 1760

Dear friend, [John Smith, of Burlington]

After I left home I heard not from my family till I came to Newport Yearly Meeting at which I received two letters from thee, dated 18: & 25: 5mo., and how acceptable they were is hard to express.

---

32. The "young woman" is not identified, *AMG*, 62.

Some part of thy first and longest letter has had a particular and frequent place in my consideration, and I think has done me a little good. I was helped with a little help.

The Yearly Meeting is now finished. E.S. and H.F. are going to Boston and eastward. J. Storer expects to visit some monthly meetings round about New York. M.R., S.E. and I expect to go to Nantucket Yearly Meeting, if way open.[33]

I find no memorial in any records in this Yearly Meeting, but now at this sitting friends have made a minute in the Yearly Meeting book, a copy to be sent to the Quarters & c., to do that work.

Thy kindness in sending my letters is gratefully owned. Truth is the same in all places: it is felt and owned by multitudes of people who yet are distinguished by some circumstances (some indeed do not live up to what they see to be right), and the clearer the discovery, the stronger to labour in that spirit which suffers long and is kind, thereby if haply to point out the more perfect way.

I have had to admire that wisdom who appoints to his servants their several and respective employments, and to adore that power which hath supported my soul and kept me in a resignation through some uncommon exercises. I remember you often with much nearness, and also my dear friends about home.

4.

Newport 17 6 1760

Dear Brother, [Abner Woolman]

I have remembered (since I left home) thee and thy family very often with much warmness of love.

We are at Newport and expect to go for Nantucket soon, if way open. We have been fellow feelers with the afflicted, nor is any affliction too great

---

33.   E.S. is identified by Gummere as Elizabeth Shipley. *AMG*, 63, note 2, see also pp. 539–540; J. Storer is John Storer, *AMG*, 63, see also p. 541; M.R. is identified by Gummere as Mary Ridgway. *AMG*, 63, note 4, see also p. 54; but is most likely Mercy Redman. *AMG*, 587; S.E. is Samuel Eastburn. *AMG*, 63, note 5, see also p. 538.

to endure for the Truth. This I own, and am labouring daily to be found in that resignation.

I am pinched for time, but wanted to let thee know I often thought of you.

John Woolman

5.

Dartmouth 23 6 1760

Dear wife,

I received thy two letters at Newport dated the 19 and 20 of the month.

And how acceptable they were to me is not easy to express. I wrote from Newport about a week past and expecting tomorrow if the wind is fair and way open to sail for Nantucket, was desirous to leave a few lines to be forwarded by any opportunity. We have been at five meetings since the Yearly Meeting and I may say by experience the Lord is good: he is a stronghold in the day of trouble and helpeth those who humbly trust in him. E. Shipley and H. Foster are gone for Boston and eastward. A. Gauntt and M.R. expect to sail for Nantucket.[34] J. Storer is in these parts and all middling well. People in these parts are generally favoured with health. I have heard very little of the small pox since I came off Long Island.

I am not so hearty and healthy as I have been sometimes, and yet through the mercy of the Almighty I am enabled to pursue our journey without much difficulty on that account.

Every year brings additional experience and I think I never more clearly saw the reasonableness and fitness of casting all my cares on God than I have since I left thee.

I remember thee and my child with endeared love and tenderness knowing how much you miss me.

I remember also that God is wise; he knows what is for the best. He is good and willing to make us as happy as we are capable of being.

He is strong and nothing is hard for him; that to love him and serve him in sincerity is the best way for us in this world. He is high and inhabits

---

34. Ann Gauntt. *AMG*, 540–41.

eternity, and dwells also with them that are poor and of a contrite spirit. Trust him, my dear, and I fear not thou'll do well.

John Woolman
I name none of my dear Friends, but my love is to them all.

6.

12th day, 12th month, at night, 1760

[to Jane Crosfield]

Since I understand thy draft toward New England at this season of the year, I have felt a near sympathy in my mind toward thee, and also thy new companion, H[annah] White.

Looking seriously over the stages and wide waters and thinking on the hard frosts and high winds usual in the winter, the journey appeared difficult; but my mind was turned to him who made and commands the winds and the waters, and whose providence is over the ravens and the sparrows.

I believe thou understood his language, and I trust thy ear will be attentive to him, and in that there is safety in the greatest difficulties. "He that believeth maketh not haste," and there seemed a hint in my mind to give thee, that thou take a sufficient portion of that doctrine along with thee on this journey. Should frozen rivers or high winds or storms sometimes prevent thou going forward so fast as thou could desire, it may be thou may find a service in tarrying even amongst a people whose company may not be every way agreeable. I remembered that the manner in which Paul made a visit to the island of Melita was contrary to his own mind as a man; we find, however, that by means thereof, the father of Publius was healed of his fever, and many cured of their infirmities.[35]

Farewell, my dear Friend
John Woolman
The want of a suitable opportunity this evening occasioned me to take this way.

---

35. For Paul's visit to Melita and his healing of the father of Publius, see Acts 28:1-9.

Letters 7–10 relate to Woolman's visit to the Delaware Indians at Wyalusing. It is interesting to read them along with the account in The Journal *chapter 8 and his notes on the earlier visit of the Delawares to Philadelphia (see Other Writings by John Woolman).*

7.

8: 6: 1763 about sunset

[To his wife, Sarah Woolman]

I am now at Bethlehem, a Moravian town, and middling well, in company with John Pemberton, William Lightfoot, and Benjamin Parvin. John expects to go toward home in the morning (it being now near night). William and Benjamin expect to go forward to Fort Allen on the frontier. Then William expects to turn home. And as to Benjamin—his mind at present seems so engaged that he shows no inclination to leave me. I have had some weighty conversation with him and let him know that I am quite free to go alone if his way does not appear clear to him. My Indian companions appear friendly and show I think quite as much regard for me as they did at our first meeting in Philadelphia. There is nothing to me that appears anyways discouraging more than what thou knew of when I was with thee. I am humbly thankful to the Lord that my mind is so supported in a trust in him that I go cheerfully on my journey and at present apprehend that I have nothing in any way to fear but a spirit of disobedience, which I trust through divine help I may be delivered from.

That pure light which enlightens every man coming into the world to me appears as lovely as ever, to the guidance of which I hope thou and I may attend while we live in this world, and then all will be well.

With endeared love to thee and my daughter and my dear friends and neighbours, I conclude, thy most affectionate

Husband John Woolman
My companions express a sympathizing love to thee.

The letter that follows is written by one of those who started on the journey with Woolman, and is addressed to Sarah Woolman, to reassure her about the safety and progress of her husband.

8.

Pikeland 6th month 13, 1763

Esteemed Friend Sarah Woolman,

I may hereby inform thee that I met thy husband at Samuel Foulk's last third day evening, and in discourse concerning the journey, he expressed a close exercise which the news of the troubles to the westward had brought upon him. Signifying that in case the journey should be attended with danger from an enemy, he thought he could be much easier to go alone than to be instrumental in bringing any into danger, who had no weightier motive to undertake it than to accompany him, and as I never had resolved on going, it seemed most easy for me to decline it. Though not much on the account of danger having heard these reports some time before without any great apprehensions of that, and am in hopes that thy husband and Benjamin Parvin (who is gone with him), may return safe again. I went with them about 20 miles beyond Bethlehem and when I parted with them, (which was the last 6th day morning) they seemed well and cheerful.

And tho' the journey may be [illegible]…occurrence, which perhaps may be a close exercise to thee on thy husband's account, yet I hope thou may be enabled to bear with patience and resignation the dispensations that providence may permit thee to pass through. I conclude thy sympathizing friend,

William Lightfoot, Jur.

P. S. B. Parvin not having time to write thee, desired me to remember his love to thee.

9.

[No date but after 16: 6: 1763]

My dear and tender Wife,

A sense of all sufficiency of God in supporting those who trust in him in all the dispensations of his providence wherein they may be tried feels comfortable in my journey.

My daily labour is to find a full resignedness to him and may say with thankfulness he remains to be my gracious father.

To him I recommend thee, my dear companion, greatly desiring thy mind may be resigned to him for I verily believe if we keep in this frame all will end well.

I write in haste but remember my dear daughter and friends.

John Woolman

In margin: "Please send this to wife."

For Israel Pemberton in Philadelphia to the care of the storekeeper at Shamokin.

10.

Burlington, 27 6 1763 1 o'clock

Dear Friend, [to Israel Pemberton]

Through the mercies of the Lord, my beloved companion and helpmate Benjamin Parvin and I were helped to perform our journey to Wahalousing and came back to Bethlehem on seventh day night, was yesterday at John Cadwaladers, and am now hasting home—Our journey though attended with much deep exercise hath been greatly to our satisfaction. We were at seven religious meetings with the Indians, many of which people, I believe, were in these troublous times greatly comforted in our visit, and they all appeared kind and loving to us—I saw nothing amongst any of them in that place which to me appeared like disaffection to the English—but our conversation was mostly with the soberer sort. The Moravian preacher who was there when I went and continued there while I stayed appeared kind and courteous from first to last, and I believe his intentions are honest.

In a humbling sense of his goodness in whom my poor soul has trusted, I remain with kind love to thee and thy family and all my dear friends.

John Woolman
For Israel Pemberton in Philadelphia

Letters 11 and 12 were printed in the first issue of the Friends Miscellany, 1831. They differ from most of Woolman's letters in being less personal and more concerned with social and economic issues. They illustrate Woolman's ability to see connections and to deal with several subjects in a single piece of writing. Readers of The Journal *will notice in the first letter the reference to silver mines, though he is not clear about who has possession of the mines or their location. His concerns about the silver mines and the use of silver appear again in the vision near the end of* The Journal, *chapter 12.*

11.

9: 7: 1769

Beloved friend, [no name]

Since our last conversation, I have felt an increase of brotherly love, and therein a liberty to hint further to thee, how, at different times for years past, things have wrought on my mind respecting high living.

First. In some afflicting seasons abroad, as I have sat in meetings with desires to attend singly on the pure gift, I have felt that amongst my brethren grievously entangled in expensive customs, the Lord has a work for some to do, by exampling others in the simplicity as it is in Christ. 2 Cor, xi. 3. And as I have seen that a view to live high hath been a stumbling block, and that what some appeared to aim at was no higher than many, esteemed of the foremost rank in our society, lived;—there hath been a labour upon me, that in this respect the way may be cast up; and the stumbling block be taken out of the way of the people. Isa. lvii. 14. And here the inexpressible love of Christ in denying himself and enduring grief for our sakes is often before me as an example for us to follow in denying ourselves of things pleasant to our natural inclinations, that we may example others in the pure Christian life in our age.

Second. In regard to thieves, I have had many serious thoughts, and often been jealous over myself, lest by withholding from a poor man what my heavenly father may have intended for him through me, I should lay a temptation in his way to steal: and I have often felt a care that no desire for riches, or outward greatness, may prompt me to get that in my house which may create envy, and increase this difficulty.

Third. I have sometimes wrote wills for people when sick and expecting soon to leave their families, and who had but little to divide among their children: and I have so far felt a brotherly sympathy that their cares have become mine, in regard to a comfortable living for them. And here, expensive customs have often made the prospect less clear. Expensive customs, on such occasions, hath often affected me with sadness.

Fourth. The manner of taking possession of the silver mines, south-westward,—the conduct of the conquerors toward the natives,—and the miserable toil of our fellow creatures in those mines have often been the subjects of my thoughts. And though I sometimes handle silver and gold as a currency, my so doing is at times attended with pensiveness, and a care that my ears may not be stopped against further instructions. I often think on other fruitfulness of the soil where we live,—the care that hath been taken to agree with the former owners, the natives,—and the conveniences this land affords for our use,— and on the numerous oppressions there are in many places; and I feel a care that my cravings may be rightly bounded, and that no wandering desire may lead me so to strengthen the hands of the wicked, as to partake of their sins. I Tim.v. 22.

Fifth. In conversing at times with some well-disposed Friends who have been long pressed with poverty, I have thought that some outward help, more than I believed myself a steward to communicate, might be a blessing to them. And at such times, the expenses that might be saved amongst some of my brethren, without any real inconvenience to them, hath often been brought to my mind; nor have I believed myself clear, without speaking at times publicly concerning it.

Sixth. My mind is often settled on the immutability of the Divine Being, and the purity of his judgments:—and a prospect of outward distress in this part of the world hath been open before me;—and I have had to behold the blessedness of a state, in which the mind is fully subjected to the Divine

Teacher, and the confusion and perplexity of such who profess the Truth, and are not faithful to the readings of it. Nor have I ever felt pity move more evidently on my mind, than I have felt it toward children who, by their education, are led on in unnecessary expenses, and examples in seeking gain in the wisdom of this world, to support themselves therein.

John Woolman

12.
[No date]

My dear friend, [no name]

In our meeting of ministers and elders, I have several times felt the moving of Divine love among us, and to me, there appeared a preparation for profitable labours in the meeting; but the time appointed for public meetings drawing near, a straitness for time hath been felt. And in Yearly Meetings for the preservation of good order in the society, when much business hath lain before us, and weighty matters relating to the testimony of Truth being under consideration, I have sometimes felt that a care in some to get forward soon, hath prevented so weighty and deliberate a proceeding, as by some hath been desired.

Sincere hearted Friends who are concerned to wait for the counsel of Truth are often made helps to each other;—and when such from distant parts of our extensive Yearly Meeting have set their houses in order, and thus gathered in one place, I believe it is the will of our Heavenly Father that we, with a single eye to the readings of his Holy Spirit, should quietly wait on him, without hurrying in the business before us.

As my mind hath been on these things, some difficulties have arisen in my way. First, there are, thro' prevailing custom, many expenses attending our entertainment in town, which, if the readings of Truth were faithfully followed, might be lessened.

Many, under an outward show of a delicate life, are entangled in a worldly spirit, laboring to support those expensive customs which they at times feel to be a burden.

These expenses, arising from a conformity to the spirit of this world, have often lain as a heavy burden on my mind, and especially at the time of our solemn meetings: an a life truly conformable to the simplicity that is in Christ, where we may faithfully serve God without distraction, and have no interruption from that which is against the Truth, to me hath been very desirable. And, my dear friend, as the Lord, in infinite mercies, hath called us to labour at times in his vineyard, and hath I believe sometimes appointed to us different offices in his work, our opening our experience one to another in the pure feeling of charity, may be profitable.

The great Shepherd of the sheep, I believe, is preparing some to example the people in a plain simple way of living; and I feel a tender care that thou and I may abide in that, where our light may shine clear, and nothing pertaining to us have any tendency to strengthen those customs which are distinguishable from the Truth as it is in Jesus.

John Woolman

Letters 13–17 were written on shipboard or after Woolman arrived in England. They supplement and perhaps provide greater understanding of Journal *chapters 11 and 12. It is interesting to compare them to the letters in Related Writings by Contemporaries in the last section of this book. Letter 13 was to Woolman's daughter and son-in-law, John and Mary Comfort, whose first child, John, was born six weeks later.*

13.
28: 4: 1772

Dear Children,

I feel a tender care for you at this time of parting from you, and in this care my mind is turned toward the pure Light of Truth, to which if you take diligent heed I trust you will find inward support under all your trials.

My leaving you under the trying circumstances now attending you, is not without close exercise and I feel a living concern that, under these cares of business, and under bodily affliction, your minds may be brought to a humble waiting on him who is the great preserver of his people. Your loving parent

John Woolman

14.

13: 6: 1772

Dear Wife,

Through the mercies of the Lord I arrived safely in London on the 8th day, 6th month. I was mercifully helped to bear the difficulties of the sea, and went straight from the waterside into the yearly meeting of ministers and elders after it was settled in the morning: and the meeting of business was first opened the same day in the afternoon. My heart hath been often melted into contrition since I left thee under a sense of divine goodness being extended for my help and preparing in me a subjection to his will. I have been comforted in the company of some sincere hearted Friends. The yearly meeting of business ended about three hours ago, and I have thoughts of going in a few days out of this city towards Yorkshire: taking some meetings in my way, if strengthened thereto.

The tender concern which I have many times felt for thee, and for Mary and John, and even for Betsy, I may not easily express. I have often remembered you with tears; and my desires have been that the Lord, who hath been my helper through many adversities, may be a father to you, and that in his love, you may be guided safely along.

Robert Willis, Sarah Morris and companion, W. Hunt and companion, and Samuel Emlen, all are here and middling well, Robert, going, I expect, for Ireland, and W. Hunt and companion, I expect, for Holland. Several friends remember kind love to thee. My kind love is to my dear friends.

John Woolman

15.

31: 7: 1772

My dear wife,

Though I feel in a good degree resigned in being absent from you, my heart is often tenderly affected toward you, and even to weeping this morning, while I am about to write.

The numerous difficulties attending us in this life are often before me, and I often remember thee with tender desires that the Holy Spirit may be thy leader, and my leader through life, and that at last we may enter into rest.

My journey hath been through inward watchfulness. I see but a little way at a time, but the Lord hath been gracious to me, and way opens for my visit in these parts.

Thy loving husband
John Woolman
about 160 miles northward from London

Letter 16 was addressed to the family of Woolman's son-in-law, John Comfort.

16.

To the children of Stephen Comfort of Bucks County:

I am now, this 16th 9th month, 1772, at Robert Proud's in Yorkshire, so well as to continue travelling, though but slowly.[36]

Yesterday, as I was walking over a plain on my way to this place, I felt a degree of divine love attend my mind, and therein an openness toward the children of Stephen Comfort, of which I believed I should endeavour to inform them. My mind was opened to behold the happiness, the safety and beauty of a life devoted to follow the heavenly shepherd; and a care that the enticements of vain young people may not ensnare any of you.

I cannot form a concern, but when a concern cometh, I endeavour to be obedient.

John Woolman

---

36. Robert Proud, a travelling minister, had been in America during 1761–62, and thus he is mentioned in letters by other travelling ministers such as William Hunt, Robert Willis, and Deborah Morris. Henry J. Cadbury, *John Woolman in England 1772: A Documentary Supplement*, 109.

The following was one of Woolman's last letters (Cadbury 111). *The cousins were Reuben and Margaret Haines* (AMG 141).

17.
23: 9: 1772

Beloved Cousins:

I am now at York at a quarterly meeting, so well in health as to continue travelling. I appoint a few meetings, but not so fast as I did some time ago. I feel quiet in my mind, believing that it is the Lord's will that I should for a time be in this part of the world. I often remember you and friends in your parts, as I pass along in this journey, and the truth as it is separate from all mixture. The Truth as it is in Jesus was never more precious to me than I feel it in this my sojourning; in which my mind is often deeply affected with that which is not of the Father but of the world. I hear that dear W. Hunt departed this life with the small pox, 9: 9: 1772 and that some of his last words were: The Truth is Over All.[37] The rest of the America Friends on the visit were lately living, and mostly middling well so far as I hear.

I left my bed and some things on board the ship I came in, directing the people to convey them to you if they arrive safe at Philadelphia.

John Woolman

---

37. William Hunt of North Carolina, another minister travelling in England, Scotland, Ireland, and Holland, died of smallpox on September 9, 1772, slightly less than one month before Woolman. *AMG,* 519; Cadbury, 7–9.

Selections From

Woolman's Essays

John Woolman is best known for his Journal, *but he also wrote a number of essays. Three of these, "Some Considerations on the Keeping of Negroes" (1754), "Considerations on Keeping Negroes, Part Second" (1762), and "A Plea for the Poor or a Word of Remembrance and Caution to the Rich" (first published 1793) are available in Phillips Moulton's* The Journal and Major Essays of John Woolman. *Two essays with various parts, "Serious Considerations on Various Subjects of Importance" (published in 1773), and "Remarks on Sundry Subjects" (written on shipboard and in England, and published in 1773), are included here as examples of later writings. There are, in addition, a number of separate essays, "On Trade," which may have been written in 1757, "Considerations on the True Harmony of Mankind," 1770, and "Concerning the Ministry," which was written in England in 1772. We have included in this* Source Book *excerpts from "Serious Considerations" and "Remarks on Sundry Subjects," and all of the essay "Concerning the Ministry."*

It is difficult to determine the exact chronology of Woolman's essays and hence to follow the development of his thought and writing style. It is generally assumed, for example, that Woolman was writing "A Plea" in 1763, the year he visited the Delawares at Wyalusing, but the essay was not published until thirty years later. The date of the early collection, "Serious Considerations on Trade," is in some doubt. The earliest extant edition bears the date 1768, but Amelia Mott Gummere suggests that it may have appeared ten years earlier, and argues that the essay "On Trade" was intended for the collection, but not published until her edition in 1922 (AMG 382, 397). Others have speculated that "On Schools," which appears in the Gummere edition (390–92) may have been written and circulated at least in manuscript form before the establishment of the school in Mt. Holly, where Woolman appears to have taught, off and on, beginning in 1759.

Despite these uncertainties, the essays can deepen our understanding of Woolman. In his Journal, *Woolman speaks frequently of laboring with people, slave owners and others, and of speaking in meetings, but he rarely tells us what he said, and how he said it. What did it mean to address the "witness" in others? The essays, along with* Conversations on the True Harmony of Mankind *that we included among "Woolman's Other Writings," give us some indication of his thought processes, his use of logic and his approach to reasoning with people. We know that he was concerned when he entered into discussions not to break the human connection with the people with whom he labored. The written word is obviously different from a face-to-face* conversation, or a "message" spoken in a meeting for worship, but essays may help us understand how Woolman worked, and how he related to other people.

The brief essay "Concerning the Ministry" was published by Amelia Mott Gummere at the end of her edition of Woolman's Journal. She says of her decision to add it to the end of The Journal, "It is retained here, apart from the Essays, as a portion of The Journal proper, because of personal references, and the light which it casts upon Woolman's travels and his state of mind" (AMG 313, note 2). She explains that the manuscript was located at Almery Garth, York, England, along with other essays by Woolman. When Phillips Moulton edited his edition of The Journal and Major Essays, however, the manuscript seemed to be lost, and he chose not to include this essay. Fortunately, a copy of the manuscript was recently located in the Library of the Society of Friends, London. We have chosen to print the essay in the Source Book because it reveals much about Woolman's late ideas on ministry, as well as on discerning one's direction and inner guidance.

Woolman, who advised his readers to "consider the connection of things" (PM 247), was himself very much aware of connections. Almost every one of his longer essays, whatever its title, deals with a number of subjects. Even individual sentences are likely to relate one issue to others. The reader may, however, discover some changes in emphasis, some development of thought, especially as Woolman added to his own experience and as the situation around him changed. It is useful to think about his essays in relation to The Journal, and to events in his own life, and in the world around him, as they are very briefly mentioned in the chronologies at the beginning of the Source Book. It is also useful to look at other materials included in the Source Book, comparing "On Schools" for example with Woolman's primer, A First Book for Children, in "Other Writings by John Woolman," and with The New England Primer, which is not included here.

from "A Plea for the Poor"

Chapter Three

While our strength and spirits are lively, we go cheerfully through business. Either too much or too little action is tiresome, but a right portion is healthful to our bodies and agreeable to an honest mind.

Where men have great estates they stand in a place of trust. To have it in their power without difficulty to live in that fashion which occasions much labour, and at the same time confine themselves to that use of things prescribed by our Redeemer, and confirmed by his example and the example of many who lived in the early ages of the Christian church, that they may more extensively relieve objects of charity—for men possessed of great estates to live thus—requires close attention to divine love.

Our gracious Creator cares and provides for all his creatures. His tender mercies are over all his works; and so far as his love influences our minds, so far we become interested in his workmanship and feel a desire to take hold of every opportunity to lessen the distresses of the afflicted and increase the happiness of the creation. Here we have a prospect of one common interest from which our own is inseparable—that to turn all the treasures we possess into the channel of universal love becomes the business of our lives.[38] Men of large estates whose hearts are thus enlarged are like fathers to the poor, and in looking over their brethren in distressed circumstances and considering their own more easy condition, find a field for humble meditation and feel the strength of those obligations they are under to be kind and tender-hearted toward them.

Poor men eased of their burdens and released from too close an application to business are at liberty to hire others to their assistance, to provide well for their animals, and find time to perform those visits amongst their acquaintance which belongs to a well-guided social life.

When these reflect on the opportunity those had to oppress them, and consider the goodness of their conduct, they behold it lovely and consistent with brotherhood; and as the man whose mind is conformed to universal love hath his trust settled in God and finds a firm foundation to stand on in any changes or revolutions that happen amongst men, so also the goodness of his conduct tends to spread a kind, benevolent disposition in the world.

---

38. Phillips Moulton in his study of the manuscripts of "A Plea for the Poor" notes that "Woolman changed 'our business' to 'the business of our lives,' thus indicating the primary importance of the imperative to which he referred. Also, 'all the treasures we possess' replaces an earlier phrase which cannot be deciphered. Perhaps this change had the same intent." *PM*, 241, note 6.

Chapter Five

To pass through a series of hardships and to languish under oppression brings people to a certain knowledge of these things. To enforce the duty of tenderness to the poor, the inspired Lawgiver referred the children of Israel to their own past experience: "Ye know the heart of a stranger, seeing ye were strangers in the land of Egypt" [Exod. 23:9]. He who hath been a stranger amongst unkind people or under their government who were hard-hearted, knows how it feels; but a person who hath never felt the weight of misapplied power comes not to this knowledge but by an inward tenderness, in which the heart is prepared to sympathy with others.

We may reflect on the condition of a poor, innocent man, who by his labour contributes toward supporting one of his own species more wealthy than himself, on whom the rich man from a desire after wealth and luxuries lays heavy burdens. When this labourer looks over the means of his heavy load, and considers that this great toil and fatigue is laid on him to support that which hath no foundation in pure wisdom, we may well suppose that there ariseth an uneasiness in his mind toward those who might without any inconvenience deal more favourably with him. When he considers that by his industry his fellow creature is benefited, and sees that this man who hath much wealth is not satisfied with being supported in a plain way—but to gratify a wrong desire and conform to wrong customs, increaseth to an extreme the labours of those who occupy his estate—we may reasonably judge that he will think himself unkindly used.

When he considers that the proceedings of the wealthy are agreeable to the customs of the times, and sees no means of redress in this world, how would the inward sighing of an innocent person ascend to the throne of that great, good Being, who created us all and hath a constant care over his creatures. By candidly considering these things, we may have some sense of the condition of innocent people overloaded by the wealthy. But he who toils one year after another to furnish others with wealth and superfluities, who labours and thinks, and thinks and labours, till by overmuch labour he is wearied and oppressed, such an one understands the meaning of that language: "Ye know the heart of a stranger, seeing ye were strangers in the land of Egypt."

As many at this day who know not the heart of a stranger indulge themselves in ways of life which occasions more labour in the world than Infinite Goodness intends for man, and yet are compassionate toward such in distress who comes directly under their observation, were these to change circumstances a while with some who labour for them, were they to pass regularly through the means of knowing the heart of a stranger and come to a feeling knowledge of the straits and hardships which many poor, innocent people pass through in a hidden obscure life, were these who now fare sumptuously every day to act the other part of the scene till seven times had passed over them, and return again to their former estate, I believe many of them would embrace a way of life less expensive and lighten the heavy burdens of some who now labour out of their sight to support them and pass through straits with which they are but little acquainted.

To see our fellow creatures under difficulties to which we are in no degree accessory tends to awaken tenderness in the minds of all reasonable people, but if we consider the condition of such who are depressed in answering our demands, who labour out of our sight and are often toiling for us while we pass our time in fullness, if we consider that much less than we demand would supply us with all things really needful, what heart will not relent, or what reasonable man can refrain from mitigating that grief which he himself is the cause of, when he may do it without inconvenience? I shall conclude with the words of Ezekiel the prophet (Chap. 34, verse 18), "Seemeth it a small…" etc. ["thing unto you to have eaten up the poor pasture, but ye must tread down with your feet the residue of your pastures?"].

"Serious Considerations On Trade"

1.

As it hath pleased the Divine Being to people the earth by inhabitants descended from one man; and as Christ commanded his disciples to preach the gospel to distant countries, the necessity of sometimes crossing the seas is evident.

2.

The inhabitants of the earth have often appeared to me as one great family consisting of various parts, divided by great waters, but united in one common interest, that is, in living righteously according to that light and understanding, wherewith Christ doth enlighten every man that cometh into the world.

3.

While a wilderness is improving, by inhabitants come from a plentiful thick settled country, to employ some of the family in crossing the waters, to supply the new settlers, with some such necessaries as they can well pay for, while they clear fields to raise grain, appears to be consistent with the interest of all—

4.

When lands are so improved that with a divine blessing they afford food, raiment, and all those necessaries which pertain to the life of a humble follower of Christ; it behooves the inhabitants to take heed that a custom be not continued longer than the usefulness of it and that the number of that calling who have been helpful in importing necessaries be not greater than is consistent with pure wisdom.

5.

Customs contrary to pure wisdom, which tends to change agreeable employ into a toil, and to involve people into many difficulties, it appears to be the duty of the fathers in the family, to wait for strength, to labour against such customs being introduced, or encouraged amongst the inhabitants; and that all true friends to the family so shake their hands from holding bribes, as not to cherish any desire of gain, by fetching, or selling, those things which they believe tend to alienate the minds of people from their truest interest.

6.

Where some have got large possessions, and by an increase of inhabitants have power to acquire riches, if they let them at such a rate that their tenants are necessitated in procuring their rent to labour harder or apply themselves to business more closely, than is consistent with pure wisdom, whither these monies thus obtained, are applied to promote a superfluous trade, or any other purpose in a self pleasing will, here the true harmony of the family appears to be in danger.

7.

Where two branches of the same family are each situated on such a soil, that with moderate labour, through the divine blessing, each may be supplied by their own produce with all the necessaries of life, and a large hazardous ocean between them; for the inhabitants of each place to live on the produce of their own land, appears most likely for them to shun unnecessary cares and labours.

8.

For brethren to visit each other in true love, I believe makes part of that happiness which our heavenly father intends for us in this life; but where pure wisdom direct not our visits, we may not suppose them truly profitable; and for man to so faithfully attend to the pure light, as to be truly acquainted with the state of his own mind, and feel that purifying power which prepares the heart to have fellowship with Christ, and with those who are redeemed from the spirit of this world, this knowledge is to us of infinitely greater moment than the knowledge of affairs in distant parts of this great family.

9.

By giving way to a desire after delicacies, and things fetched far, many men appear to be employed unnecessarily; many ships built by much labour are lost; many people brought to an untimely end; much good produce buried in the seas; many people busied in that which serves chiefly to please a wandering desire, who might better be employed in those affairs which are of real service, and ease the burdens of such poor honest people, who to answer the demands of others are often necessitated to exceed the bounds of healthful agreeable exercise.

10.

Blessed are the peace makers for they shall be called the children of GOD.

Where one in the family is injured, it appears consistent with true brotherhood, that such who know it, take due care respecting their own behavior, and conduct, lest the love of gain should lead them into any affairs, so connected with the proceedings of him who doth the injury, as to strengthen his hands therein, make him more at ease in a wrong way, or less likely to attend to the righteous principle in his own mind.

11.

To be well acquainted with the affairs we are interested in, with the disposition of those with whom we have connections, to have outward concerns within proper bounds, and in all things attend to the wisdom from above, appears most agreeable to that pious disposition in which people desire to shun doubtful disputes about property, to have their proceedings so agreeable to righteousness, that whatsoever they do, they may do all to the glory of God, and give none offence, neither to the Jews, nor to the gentiles, nor to the church of Christ.

12.

Where men give way to a desire after wealth, and to obtain their ends proceed in that wisdom which is from beneath, how often does discord arise between different branches of the great family? whence great numbers of men are often separated from tilling the earth, and useful employ, to defend what contending parties mutually claim as their interest; hence many are cut off in youth and great troubles and devastations do often attend these contests; and besides those sorrowful circumstances, the food these armies eat, the garments they wear, their wages, vessels to transport them from place to place, and support for the maimed, tends to increase the labour of such who fill the earth, and to make some employments necessary which without wars would not; here that healthful agreeable exercise, which I believe our gracious creator intended for us, is often changed into hurry and toil.

O how precious is the spirit of peace! how desirable that state in which people feel their hearts humbly resigned to the Lord, and live under a labour of mind to do his will on earth as it is done in heaven. Where they feel content with that true simplicity in which no wandering desires leads on to strife, where no treasures possessed in a selfish spirit, tends to beget ill will in other selfish men. And where true love so seasons their proceedings, that the pure witness is reached in such who are well acquainted with them.

From "Serious Considerations on Various Subjects of Importance (On Schools)"[39]

"Suffer the little children to come unto me, and forbid them not, for of such is the kingdom of God." Mark 10:14.

To encourage children to do things with a view to get praise of men, to me appears an obstruction to their being inwardly acquainted with the spirit of Truth. For it is the work of the Holy Spirit to direct the mind to God, that in all our proceedings we may have a single eye to him to give alms in secret, to fast in secret, and labour to keep clear of that disposition reproved by our Savior, "But all their works they do for to be seen of men." Matt. 23:5.

That divine light which enlightens all men, I believe, does often shine in the minds of children very early; and to humbly wait for wisdom, that our conduct toward them may tend to forward their acquaintance with it, and strengthen them in obedience thereto, appears to me to be a duty on all of us.

By cherishing the spirit of pride and the love of praise in them, I believe they may sometimes improve faster in learning, than otherwise they would; but to take measures to forward children in learning, which naturally tend to divert their minds from true humility, appears to me to savour of the wisdom of this world.

If tutors are not acquainted with sanctification of spirit, nor experienced in an humble waiting for the leadings of Truth, but follow the maxims of the wisdom of this world, such children who are under their tuition, appear to me to be in danger of imbibing thoughts and apprehensions, reverse to that meekness and lowliness of heart, which is necessary for all the true followers of Christ.

---

39.   It is interesting to compare this essay with Woolman's other short essay, "On Schools" which comprises chapter 14 of "A Plea for the Poor." *PM,* 263.

Children at an age fit for schools, are in a time of life which requires the patient attention of pious people, and if we commit them to the tuition of such, whose minds we believe are not rightly prepared to "train them up in the nurture and admonition of the Lord," we are in danger of not acting the part of faithful parents toward them; for our Heavenly Father doth not require us to do evil, that good may come of it. And it is needful that we deeply examine ourselves, lest we get entangled in the wisdom of this world, and, through wrong apprehensions, take such methods in education as may prove a great injury to the minds of our children.

It is a lovely sight to behold innocent children and when they are sent to such schools, where their tender minds are in imminent danger of being led astray by tutors who do not live a self-denying life, or by the conversation of such children who do not live in innocence, it is a case much to be lamented.

While a pious tutor hath the charge of no more children than he can take due care of, and keeps his authority in the Truth, the good spirit in which he leads and governs, works on the minds of such who are not hardened, and his labours not only tend to bring them forward in outward learning, but to open their understandings with respect to the true Christian life. But where a person hath charge of too many, and his thoughts and time are so much employed in the outward affairs of his school, that he does not so weightily attend to the spirit and conduct of each individual, as to be enabled to administer rightly to all in due season; through such omission, he not only suffers as to the state of his own mind, but the minds of the children are in danger of suffering also.

To watch the spirit of children, to nurture them in gospel love, and labour to help them against that which would mar the beauty of their minds, is a debt we owe them: and a faithful performance of our duty, not only tends to their lasting benefit and our own peace, but also to render their company agreeable to us.

Instruction, thus administered, reaches the pure witness in the minds of such children who are not hardened, and begets love in them toward those who thus lead them on. But where too great a number are committed to a tutor, and he, through much cumber, omits a careful attention to the minds of children, there is danger of disorders gradually increasing amongst them, till the effects thereof appear in their conduct, too strong to be easily remedied.

A care hath lived on my mind, that more time might be employed by parents at home, and by tutors at school, in weightily attending to the spirit and inclinations of children, and that we may so lead, instruct, and govern them, in this tender part of life, that nothing may be omitted in our power, to help them on their way to become the children of our Father who is in Heaven.

Meditating on the situation of schools in our provinces, my mind hath, at times, been affected with sorrow; and under these exercises it hath appeared to me, that if those who have large estates, were faithful stewards, and laid no rent nor interest, nor other demand, higher than is consistent with universal love; and those in lower circumstances would, under a moderate employ, shun unnecessary expense, even to the smallest article; and all unite in humbly seeking to the Lord, he would graciously instruct us, and strengthen us, to relieve the youth from various snares, in which many of them are entangled.[40]

From "Remarks on Sundry Subjects"

On Loving Our Neighbors as Ourselves

As I have travelled in England, I have had a tender feeling of the condition of poor people, some of whom though honest and industrious, have nothing to spare for the schooling of their children.

There is a proportion between labour and the necessaries of life, and, in true brotherly love, the mind is open to feel after the necessities of the poor.

Amongst the poor there are some that are weak through age and others of a weakly nature, who pass through straits in very private life, without asking relief from the public.

Such who are strong and healthy may do that business which to the weakly may be oppressive; and in performing that in a day which is esteemed a

---

40. Woolman's observations of the interrelated "connection of things" can be seen here between the luxuries of the wealthy, high rents imposed upon the poor, and the subtle, injurious effects for children.

day's labour, by weakly persons in the field and in the shops, and by weakly women who spin and knit in the manufactories, they often pass through weariness; and many sighs I believe are uttered in secret, unheard by some who might ease their burdens.

Labour in the right medium is healthy, but in too much of it there is a painful weariness; and the hardships of the poor are sometimes increased through want of more agreeable nourishment, more plentiful fuel for the fire, and warmer clothing in the winter than their wages will answer.

When I have beheld plenty in some houses to a degree of luxury, the condition of poor children brought up without learning, and the condition of the weakly and aged, who try to live by their labour, hath often revived in my mind, as cases of which some who live in fullness need to be put in remembrance.

There are few, if any, who could behold their fellow creatures lie long in distress and forebear to help them, when they could do it without any inconvenience; but customs requiring much labour to support them, do often lie heavy on the poor, while they who live in these customs are so entangled in a multitude of unnecessary concerns, that they think but little of the hardships which the poor people go through....

When our will is subject to the will of God, and in relation to the things of this world we have nothing in view but a comfortable living equally with the rest of our fellow creatures, then outward treasures are no further desirable than as we feel a gift in our minds equal to the trust, and strength to act as dutiful children in his service who hath formed all mankind, and appointed a subsistence for us in this world.

A desire for treasures on any other motive appears to be against that command of our blessed Savior, Lay not up for yourselves treasures here on earth, Matt 6:19.

He forbids not laying up in the summer for the wants of winter; nor doth he teach us to be slothful in that which properly relates to our being in this world: but in this prohibition he puts in yourselves. Lay not up for yourselves treasures here on earth.

Now in the pure light, this language is understood, for in the love of Christ there is no respect of persons, and while we abide in his love we live not to ourselves, but to him who died for us. And as we are thus united in spirit to Christ, we are engaged to labour in promoting that work in the earth for which he suffered....

In the harmonious spirit of society, Christ is all in all [Col. 3:11].

Here it is that old things are passed away, all things are new, all things are of God; and the desire for outward riches is at an end.

They of low degree who have small gifts enjoy their help who have large gifts; those with small gifts have a small degree of care, while those with their large gifts have a large degree of care: and thus to abide in the love of Christ and enjoy a comfortable living in this world is all that is aimed at by those members in society to whom Christ is made wisdom and righteousness.

But when they who have much treasure, are not faithful stewards of the gifts of God, great difficulties attend it.

Now this matter hath deeply affected my mind. The Lord, through merciful chastisements, hath given me a feeling of that love, in which the harmony of society doth stand, and a sight of the growth of that seed which bringeth forth wars and great calamities in the world, and a labour attends me to open it to others....

On the Slave Trade

Through departing from the Truth as it is in Jesus, through introducing ways of life attended with unnecessary expenses, many wants have arisen, the minds of people have been employed in studying to get wealth, and in this pursuit, some departing from equity, have retained a profession of religion; others have looked at their example, and thereby been strengthened to proceed further in the same way; thus many have encouraged the trade of taking men from Africa and selling them as slaves.

It hath been computed that near one hundred thousand Negroes have, of late years, been taken annually from the coast by ships employed in the English trade.

As I have travelled on religious visits in some parts of America, I have seen many of these people under the command of overseers, in a painful servitude.

I have beheld them as gentiles, under people professing Christianity, not only kept ignorant of the Holy Scriptures, but under great provocations to wrath, of whom it may truly be said, They that rule over them make them to howl, and the Holy Name is abundantly blasphemed, [Isa. 52:5]. Where children are taught to read the sacred writings while young, and exampled in meekness and humility, it is often helpful to them; nor is this any more than a debt due from us to a succeeding age.

But where youth are pinched for want of the necessaries of life, forced to labour under the harsh rebukes of rigorous overseers, and many times endure unmerciful whippings; in such an education, how great are the disadvantages they lie under! And how forcibly do these things work against the increase of the government of the Prince of Peace!...

I have read some books wrote by people who were personally acquainted with the manner of getting slaves in Africa.

I have had verbal relations of this nature from several Negroes brought from Africa, who have learned to talk English.

I have sundry times heard Englishmen speak on this subject, who have been in Africa on this business, and from all these accounts, it appears evident that great violence is committed, and much blood shed in Africa in getting slaves.

When three or four hundred slaves are put in the hold of a vessel in a hot climate, their breathing soon affects the air. Were that number of free people to go passengers, with all things proper for their voyage, there would inconvenience arise from the greatness of their number; but slaves are taken by violence, and frequently endeavour to kill the white people, that they may return to their native land. Hence they are frequently kept under some sort of confinement, by means of which a scent arises in the hold of the ship, and distempers often break out amongst them, of which many die. Of this tainted air in the hold of ships freighted with slaves, I have had several accounts, some of them in print, and some verbal, and all agree that the scent is grievous. When these people are sold in America and in the islands, they are commonly made to labour in a manner more servile and constant than that they were used to at home, that with grief, with different diet from what has been common with them, and with hard labour, some thousands are computed to die every year, in what is called the seasoning.

Thus it appears evident that great numbers of these people are brought every year to an untimely end, many of them being such who never injured us....

Many lives have been shortened through extreme oppression, while they laboured to support luxury and worldly greatness; and though many people in outward prosperity may think little of those things, yet the gracious Creator hath regard to the cries of the innocent, however unnoticed by men.

The Lord in the riches of his goodness is leading some unto the feeling of the condition of this people, who cannot rest without labouring as their advocates, of which in some measure I have had experience; for in the movings of his love in my heart, these poor sufferers have been brought near me....

Where a trade is carried on, productive of much misery, and they who suffer by it are some thousands of miles off, the danger is the greater of not laying their sufferings to heart.

In procuring slaves on the coast of Africa, many children are stolen privately; wars are also encouraged amongst the Negroes, but all is at a great distance.

Many groans arise from dying men, which we hear not.

Many cries are uttered by widows and fatherless children, which reach not our ears.

Many cheeks are wet with tears, and faces sad with unutterable grief, which we see not.

Cruel tyranny is encouraged. The hands of robbers are strengthened, and thousands reduced to the most abject slavery, who never injured us.

Were we for the terms of one year only to be an eye-witness to what passeth in getting these slaves;

Was the blood which is shed to be sprinkled on our garments;

Were the poor captives, bound with thongs, heavy laden with elephants teeth, to pass before our eyes on the way to the sea;

Were their bitter lamentations day after day to ring in our ears, and their mournful cries in the night to hinder us from sleeping;

Were we to hear the sound of the tumult at sea, when the slaves on board the ships attempt to kill the English, and behold the issue of these bloody conflicts;

What pious man could be a witness to these things, and see a trade carried on in this manner, without being deeply affected with sorrow?...

In the trade to Africa for slaves, and in the management of ships going on these voyages, many of our lads and young men have a considerable part of their education.

Now what pious father beholding his son in one of these ships, to learn the practice of a mariner, could forbear mourning over him?

Where youth are exampled in means of getting money, so full of violence, and used to exercise such cruelties on their fellow creatures, the disadvantage to them in their education is very great.

But I feel it in my mind to write concerning the seafaring life in general.

In the trade carried on from the West Indies, and from some part of the continent, the produce of the labour of slaves is a considerable part.

And sailors who are frequently at ports where slaves abound, and converse often with people who oppress without the appearance of remorse, and often with sailors employed in the slave trade, how powerfully do these evil examples spread amongst a seafaring youth!...

Under the humbling power of Christ, I have seen that if the leadings of the Holy Spirit were faithfully attended to by his confessed followers in general, the heathen nations would be exampled in righteousness. A less number of people would be employed on the seas. The channels of trade would be more free from defilement. Fewer people would be employed in vanities and superfluities.

The inhabitants of cities would be less in number. Those who have much lands would become fathers to the poor.

More people would be employed in the sweet employment of husbandry, and in the path of pure wisdom, labour would be an agreeable healthful employment.

"Concerning The Ministry"

On this visit to England I have felt some instructions sealed on my mind, which I am concerned to leave in writing for the use of such who are called to the station of a minister of Christ.

Christ being the Prince of Peace, and we being no more than ministers, I find it necessary for us, not only to feel a concern in our going forth, but to experience the renewing thereof in the appointment of meetings.

I felt a concern in America to prepare for this voyage; and being through the mercy of God brought safe here, my heart was like a vessel that wanted vent; and for several weeks at first, when my mouth was opened in meetings, it often felt like the raising of a gate in a water course, where a weight of water lay upon it; and in these labours there appeared a fresh visitation of love to many, especially the youth. But some time after this I felt empty and poor and yet felt a necessity to appoint meetings.

In this state I was exercised to abide in the pure life of Truth, and in all my labours to watch diligently against the motions of self in my own mind.

I have frequently felt a necessity to stand up when the spring of the ministry was low, and to speak from the necessity, in that which subjecteth the will of the creature; and herein I was united with the suffering seed, and found inward sweetness in these mortifying labours.

As I have been preserved in a watchful attention to the Divine leader under these dispensations, enlargement at times hath followed, and the power of Truth hath rose higher in some meetings than I ever knew it before through me.

Thus I have been more and more instructed as to the necessity of depending, not upon a concern which I felt in America to come on a visit to England, but upon the fresh instructions of Christ, the Prince of Peace, from day to day.[41]

Now of late, I have felt a stop in the appointment of meetings, not wholly but in part; and I do not feel liberty to appoint them so quickly one after another as I have heretofore, and I feel thankful, in that I have not noise with me, in these slow proceedings.

The work of the ministry being a work of Divine love, I feel that the openings thereof are to be waited for in all our appointments.

---

41. This passage suggests that Woolman experienced about this time a new way of understanding the inward "leadings of the spirit." Whatever his reasons for making the trip to England, which have never been fully understood, he seems at this point to have let go of long-range goals for what he perceives to be a daily renewal of direction.

Oh! how deep is Divine wisdom! Christ puts forth his ministers, and goeth before them; and Oh! how great is the danger of departing from the pure feeling of that which leadeth safely!

Christ knoweth the state of the people, and in the pure feeling of the gospel ministry, their states are opened to his servants.

Christ knoweth when the fruit-branches themselves have need of purging.

Oh! that these lessons may be remembered by me! and that all who appoint meetings may proceed in the pure feeling of duty.

I have sometimes felt a necessity to stand up; but that spirit which is of the world hath so much prevailed in many, and the pure life of Truth been so pressed down that I have gone forward, not as one travelling in a road cast up and well prepared, but as a man walking through a miry place, in which there are stones here and there safe to step on; but so situated that one step being taken, time is necessary to see where to step next.

Now I find that in pure obedience the mind learns contentment in appearing weak and foolish to that wisdom which is of the world; and in these lowly labours, they who stand in a low place, rightly exercised under the cross, will find nourishment.

The gift is pure; and while the eye is single in attending thereto, the understanding is preserved clear, self is kept out, and we rejoice in filling up that which remains of the afflictions of Christ for his body's sake, which is the church.

The natural man loveth eloquence, and many love to hear eloquent orations; and if there is not a careful attention to the gift, men who have once laboured in the pure gospel ministry, growing weary of suffering, and ashamed of appearing weak, may kindle a fire, compass themselves about with sparks, and walk in the light—not of Christ who is under suffering—but of that fire which they, going from the gift, have kindled; and that in hearers, which is gone from the meek suffering state into the worldly wisdom, may be warmed with this fire, and speak highly of these labours, and thus the false prophet in man may form likenesses and his coming may be with signs and wonders and lying miracles; and deceivableness of unrighteousness: but the sorcerers, however powerful; they remain without in company with the idolaters and adulterers. That which is of God gathers to God; and that which is of the world is owned by the world.

In this journey a labour hath attended my mind, that the ministers amongst us may be preserved in the meek feeling life of Truth, where we have no desire but to follow Christ and be with him; that when he is under suffering we may suffer with him; and never desire to rise up in dominion, but as he by the virtue of his own Spirit may raise us.

Other Writings
by Woolman

Woolman's writings do not all fit into the categories of journal, letters, and essays. He left account books, an "Epistle to the Monthly and Quarterly Meetings," a dialogue, notes, and a schoolbook. We have not included the account books, though they tell us a great deal about how Woolman made his living, nor the epistle, which is interesting as a kind of farewell message to his fellow American Quakers as he prepared to leave for England. We have included: (1) excerpts from Conversations on the True Harmony of Mankind and How It May Be Promoted; (2) Woolman's notes on a conversation with Papunehang, "The Substance of Some Conversation with Paponahoal the Indian Chief..."; and (3) his primer, A First Book for Children.

The Conversations, a kind of Socratic dialogue, was not published until 1831, when it appeared in the Friends Miscellany. It was printed again by Amelia Mott Gummere in 1922 and by the Friends World Committee in 1987. Written just before Woolman sailed for England, it was an effort to draw readers into a dialogue on economic matters. Since Woolman describes it as the "substance" of conversations he has been engaged in, it may give the reader a sense of how Woolman labored with others. The "labouring man" in the two dialogues presumably speaks Woolman's own mind.

Woolman's "The Substance of Some Conversation with Paponahoal the Indian Chief..." which exists in a one-page manuscript, helps us understand better Woolman's previous experience with Papunehang, the chief of the Wyalusing Delawares whom he visited in 1763.[42] These notes can be compared in a useful way, both with the account of the visit to Wyalusing in chapter 8 of The Journal, and with the longer account of the visit of the Indians in Philadelphia, in 1760, "Some Account of the Behaviour and Sentiments of a Number of Well-Disposed Indians," which is in the next section of the Source Book.

A First Book for Children was intended to give children the reading skills needed to read the Bible for themselves. It moves from the alphabet through very simple sentences to the story of the Good Samaritan. This primer, which is only 32 pages long, has been printed here four pages to a page. It went through at least three

---

42.   In Woolman's manuscript notes of this meeting, the complete title is not entirely legible after "the Indian Chief." It includes the words "in the presence of J.W-n" above which is written "John Woolman." The manuscript ends with a note in Sarah Ellis Woolman's handwriting verifying that the writing is her husband's. The names "Paponahoal" and "Papoonahoal" are several variant spellings of "Papunehang," which is the spelling as it appears in Woolman's Journal, chapter 8.

editions, although only one known copy of the original, in the third edition, survives. Woolman presumably used it in the school in Mt. Holly, where he probably taught between 1759 and 1769.

It is useful to compare A First Book for Children *with his essay "On Schools "(in the* Source Book*) and with* The New England Primer, *which was used very widely for more than one hundred years. By comparison with* The New England Primer, *Woolman's book expresses the Quaker objection to creeds and outward authority for it offers no real doctrine. Woolman's choice to include the story of the Good Samaritan also seems significant.* The New England Primer *took different forms in different places and times, but facsimile editions are readily available.*

from *Conversations on The True Harmony of Mankind and How It May Be Promoted*

Introduction

I have at sundry times felt my mind opened in true brotherly love, to converse freely and largely with some who were entrusted with plentiful estates, in regard to an application of the profits of them, consistent with pure wisdom. And of late, it hath often revived on my mind as a duty, to write the substance of what then passed, and as I have attended to this concern, I have felt my mind opened to enlarge on some points then spoken to.

John Woolman. mo 3: 1772

The Substance of some conversation between a labouring man, and a man rich in money:[43]

---

43. "Amelia Mott Gummere speculates that the rich man may have been a member of the Pemberton, Smith, or Morris families. Actual identifications are not important, but Gummere's speculations suggest the kinds of people with whom Woolman may have talked about economic matters. Israel Pemberton, for example, was a prominent Quaker and a business advisor to Woolman. His brother John Pemberton was a close friend…The Smiths and Morrises were members of Woolman's home meeting. Samuel Smith was a prosperous merchant and shipbuilder; John Smith carried on trade with England, Ireland, Portugal, Madeira, and the West Indies. Thus the rich man was probably someone to whom Woolman could open his mind freely and frankly, someone he knew in Meeting, someone whose home he had visited….[There are] three things in the *Conversations* which stand out: (1) a detailed investigation of what Woolman in 'A Plea for the Poor' calls 'the

Laborer speaks thus: I observe thou livest easy, as to bodily labour, and perceive thou takest interest at seven per cent. I find occasion amongst us labouring men, in supporting our families, to work harder at times than is agreeable to us, I am now thinking of that Christian exhortation, love as brethren! and propose to thee my neighbor, whether a way may not be opened for thee and thy family to live comfortably on a lower interest, which if once rightly attained, would I believe work in favour of us laboring people.

Rich. If thou payest no interest, wherein doth seven per cent affect thee?

Laborer. I was at work for a husbandman who had bought a plantation, and paid interest for a great part of the purchase money. As this neighbor and I were talking of the quantity of grain, equitable pay for a day's work, he told me that so much of the produce of his ground went yearly to pay the interest of the remaining purchase money, that he thought he could not afford as much rye for a day's work now, as was considered pay for a day's work twenty years ago.

Rich. Twenty years ago interest was as high as it is now, and grain, flesh, butter, and cheese were then cheaper.

Laborer. Seven per cent, is higher than interest is in England, and than it is in most of the neighboring provinces. This is known to many who pay interest, who look at wealthy interest receivers, as men having got an advantage of their brethren; and as the provisions are more and more in demand, partly by an enlargement of towns and villages, and partly by a sea-trade, some take hold of opportunities to raise the price of grain, flesh, butter, and the like and apprehend that herein they are only labouring to bring the price of their produce toward a balance with seven percent.

On a rise of grain, of flesh, and the like, I have known trades men meet and raise the price of their work, thus a poor labouring man who works by the day for the necessaries of life, must not only work more for a bushel of grain, but also for weaving of his cloth, for making of his coat, and for the shoes which he wears.

---

connection of things'; (2) an example of how Woolman may have labored with others; and (3) a demonstration of his concern not only for poor people and the oppressed, but also for the rich people and oppressors." Sterling Olmsted, ed., *Conversations on the True Harmony of Mankind and How It May Be Promoted,* from the editor's comments and questions, 2.

There also ariseth discouragement hereby to tradesmen, in our country in general, for tradesmen raising their wages on a rise of grain, the price of cloth, of shoes, of hats, of scythes, and the like, are all raised.

Now if Interest was lower, grain lower, and kept more plentiful in our country, wages of hired men might with reason be lower also. Hence encouragement would naturally arise to husbandmen to raise more sheep and flax, and prepare means to employ many poor people amongst us.

Sheep are pleasant company on a plantation, their looks are modest, their voice is soft and agreeable; the slowness of their run exposeth them a prey to wild beasts, and they appear to be intended by the great Creator to live under our protection, and supply us with matter for warm and useful clothing. Sheep being rightly managed tend to enrich our land; but by sending abroad great quantities of grain and flour, the fatness of our land is diminished.

I have known landholders who paid interest for large sums of money, and being intent on paying their debts by raising grain, have by too much tilling, so robbed the earth of its natural fatness, that the produce thereof hath grown light.

To till poor land requires near as much labour as to till that which is rich, and as the high interest of money which lieth on many husbandmen is often a means of their struggling for present profit, to the impoverishment of their lands, they then on their poor land find greater difficulty to afford poor laborers who work for them, equitable pay for tilling the ground.

The produce of the earth is a gift from our gracious Creator to the inhabitants, and to impoverish the earth now to support outward greatness appears to be an injury to the succeeding age.

Rich. As there hath for some years past been a gradual rise of our country produce, and we have not raised our interest, if there be any complaint now, it seems as if we are the men to complain.

Laborer. My loving friend and neighbor! People, thou knowest, sometimes disagree in attempting to settle accounts (when no fraud is intended on either side) but through want of matters being clearly and fairly stated. Come now, let us patiently hear each other, and endeavour to love as brethren.

Some who pay rent for a small house, and raise up children, all by day's labor, are often taught by very moving instructions. Some keep a cow, and labour hard in the summer to provide hay and grain for her against winter; but in very cold winters, hay is sometimes gone before spring, and grain is so scarce, through much sending of it and flour abroad, that the grain intended for a cow, is found necessary to be eaten in the family. I have known grain & hay so scarce, that I could not anywhere near get so much as my family and creatures had need of; being then sparing in feeding our cow, she hath grown poor. In her pining condition, she hath called aloud. I knew her voice, and the sound thereof was the cry of hunger. I have known snowy, stormy weather, of long continuance. I have seen poor creatures in distress, for want of good shelter and plentiful feeding, when it did not appear to be in the power of their owners to do much better for them, being straitened in answering the demands of the wealthy. I have seen small fires in long cold storms, and known sufferings for want of firewood. In wasting away under want, nature hath a voice that is very piercing. To these things I have been a witness, and had a feeling sense of them; nor may I easily forget what I have thus learned.

Now my friend I have beheld that fullness and delicacy in which thou and thy family live. Those expensive articles, brought from beyond the sea, which serve chiefly to please the desire of the eye, and to gratify the palate, which I often observe in thy family as in other rich families; these costly things are often revived in my remembrance when those piercing instructions arising from hunger and want, have been before me.

Our merchants, in paying for these delicacies, send a great deal of flour and grain abroad. Hence grain is more scarce and dear, which operates against poor laboring people.

I have seen, in thy family that in furnishing the house, in dressing yourselves, and in preparations for the table, you might save a good deal if your minds were reconciled to that simplicity mentioned by the apostle, to wit, the simplicity that there is in Christ; and thus by saving you might help poor people in several ways. You might abate of your interest money, and that might operate in favor of the poor. Your example in a plain life might encourage other rich families in this simple way of living, who, by abating their expenses, might the easier abate the rents of their lands, and their tenants, having farms on easier terms, would have less plea for shortening the wages of the poor by raising the price of grain than they now have.

I have felt hardships amongst poor people, and had experience of their difficulties; now my friend! were our stations in the world to be changed; were thou and thy children to labor a few years with your hands, under all the wants and difficulties of the poor, toward supporting us and our families in that expensive way of life in which thou and thy family now liveth, thou would see that we might have a sufficiency with much less, and on abating our demands, might make thy labor and the labor of thy children much easier, and doubtless in my case, to thee such abatement would be desirable.

I have read of a heathen king or emperor so affected with that great law of equity, laid down by our Redeemer, that he caused it to be fixed up on the wall of his palace. In that law, our Redeemer refers us to our own feelings: Whatsoever ye would that men should do to you, do you even so to them. And as all men by nature are equally entitled to the equity of this law, and under the obligations of it, there appears on the point of tenderness to the poor improvement necessary for thee, my friend.

Rich. If I were to abate all those expenses thou hintest at, I believe some poor people, as hard set to live in the world as those thou speaks of, would lose some business, and be more straitened to live than they are at present.

Laborer. I know of no employ in life, more innocent in its nature, more healthy, and more acceptable in common to the minds of honest men, than husbandry, followed no further than while action is agreeable to the body; but husbandry, by the smallness of the number employed in it is often made a toil, and the sweetness thereof changed into hurry and weariness in doing no more than tenants commonly expect from a man as the labor of a day.

Rich. I have seen men perform a full day's labor, even in hot weather, and at night appeared cheerful, and no signs of weariness on them.

Laborer. That may often be seen in strong hearty men; but sometimes the necessities of poor laboring men induce them to labor when they are weakly; and among poor men as amongst others, some are weak by nature, and not prepared to go through great labors, and these, in doing what is esteemed a day's work in the summer, are frequently very weary before night, even when in health; and when weakly, sometimes struggle with labor to a great degree of oppression.

Laboring to raise the necessaries of life, is in itself an honest labor, and the more men employed in honest employments the better.

Many of the employments thou hinteth at have been invented to gratify the wandering desires of those who, through means of riches, had power to turn money into the channels of vanity, which employments are often distressing to the minds of sincere hearted people, who from their childhood have been brought up in them, with intent that thereby they might get a living in the world. With these I have a brotherly sympathy, and not only desire that their faith fail not, but feel a care that such who have plenty of the things of this life may lay their condition to heart.

I feel that it is my duty to love my heavenly Father with all my soul and strength. I feel that pride is opposite to divine love; and if I put forth my strength in any employ which I know is to support pride, I feel that it has a tendency to weaken those bands which through the infinite mercies of God, I have felt at times to bind and unite my soul in a holy fellowship with the Father and with his Son Jesus Christ. This I have learned through the precious operation of divine love, and ardently desire both for myself, and for all who have tasted of it, that nothing may be able to separate us from it.

When rich men who have the power of circulating money through channels the most pleasant to them, do not stand upright as in the sight of God, but go forth in a way contrary to pure wisdom, it tends to disorder the affairs of society; and where they gather money through the toil of husbandmen, and circulate it by trading in superfluities, and employing people in vanities, the similitude used by the prophet Ezekiel appears applicable. He represents rich men as strong cattle, who feed on the fat pasture, and then tread down the remainder; and as drinking at a pleasant stream, and then walking in it till their feet have so stirred up the mud, that the thirsty weak cattle have nothing to drink but dirty water. And this parable of the prophet appears to represent, not only the bodily hardships, in outward poverty and want, of such poor people who are pressed down by the power of the wealthy, but may properly be applied to those employments about vanities in which many poor people are entangled.

Now if rich men by living in the simplicity of the Truth, stop the business of some who labor in gratifying the pride and vanities of people's minds, and are drinking the dirty waters;—if those at the same time abate their interest, and the rent of their lands, this opens a way for the tenant to be more liberal with the fruits of the ground, when put in the balance against the work of poor laboring men.

An honest tenant who labours himself and knows what it is to be weary, on agreeing to pay five men full wages for doing that which is now computed a day's work for four, might ease the heavy burdens of weakly laborers, and open the way for some now employed in gratifying the vanities of people's minds to enter upon useful employ.

Men who live on a supply from the interest of their money, and do little else but manage it, appear to have but a small share of the labor in carrying on the affairs of a province; and when a member of society doth but a small share of the business thereof, it appears most agreeable to equity that he should endeavor to live in such sort, as may be most easy to them by whose labour he is chiefly supported.

"The Substance of Some Conversation with Paponahoal the Indian Chief…"

Speaking on that which was the cause of frequent wars and bloodshed which so much prevailed in the world, he said that men, not keeping to that love which our Maker had given us in our hearts, the evil spirit gets possession there and destroys all that is good in us, and this is the cause why men dislike one another and grow angry with and endeavour to kill one another; but that when we follow the leadings of this good spirit it causes our hearts to be tender, to love one another, and to look upon all mankind as one family. He manifested the sense he was under of the necessity and effects of this divine love as he was speaking by a sweetness of voice, often pressing his hand against his breast.

He farther said that when at any time something arose in his mind that would persuade him that he knew more than other people, a fear would spring up in his heart lest this should occasion him to fall backward in his religious progress, which made him often to pray to his Maker to help him to keep out such thoughts and that he might be preserved in love and affection to all men, so that he might never slight nor undervalue the poor and raise nor set up the great ones, but be kept in that love which preserves the heart lowly, humble and in a respectful regard to all our fellow creatures.

That he had for many years felt the good spirit in his heart, but wanting to try and prove it he was not fully settled in that love till about four years past when he became fully satisfied that that love was good and that he need no[t] further enquire upon it, being sure that it was the right way and in that way he had endeavoured since that time steadily to walk.

That this spirit was of love and that it was his daily prayer to his Maker that it might continually abide with him, that when he felt this spirit prevail in his heart, he was preserved to speak only that which was right, and that no evil words came out of his mouth while this spirit continued in his heart.

That it was not good to speak upon matters relating to the Almighty only from the root of the tongue outward, but that in order that their words should be good they must come from the good in the heart.

He expressed his sorrow that men should make so bad a use of the breath of life which God had breathed in them, which he ought continually improve to his honour and the good of people.

He appeared in much tenderness of spirit and spoke with a particular sweetness of voice, and after a seasonable time in conversation he gravely said he had no more to say on religious subjects to us this afternoon.

> This writing in my dear husband's
> own hand if friends think them
> worth a printing I am willing
> if not I desire content.
>
> It's impaired but
> I think a good scholar
> may read it.
> I would hold nothing back
> that will be useful.

A

Firſt BOOK for Children.

Much uſeful reading being ſtudied and learn
by Children in Schools before they can read
this Book is intended to ſave unneceſſary
pence.

By JOHN WOOLMAN.

The third Edition enlarged.

ABCDEFGHIJKLMN
OPQRSTVUWXYZ

a b c d e f g h i j k l m n
o p q r ſ s t v u w x y z

Note. When the above Alphabet is defaced, this Leaf
may be paſted upon the Cover, and the Alphabet on the
other Side made uſe of.

PHILADELPHIA:
Printed, and Sold by JOSEPH CRUIKSHANK, in Second-
ſtreet; and by BENJAMIN FERRISS, Stationer and
Bookbinder, in Wilmington.

A First Book for Children, cover

ABCDEFGHIJKLMN
OPQRSTVUWXYZ

a b c d e f g h i j k l m n
o p q r ſ s t v u w x y z &

ba	be	bi	bo	bu
ca	ce	ci	co	cu
da	de	di	do	du
fa	fe	fi	fo	fu
ga	ge	gi	go	gu
ha	he	hi	ho	hu
ka	ke	ki	ko	ku
la	le	li	lo	lu
ma	me	mi	mo	mu
na	ne	ni	no	nu
pa	pe	pi	po	pu
ra	re	ri	ro	ru
ſa	ſe	ſi	ſo	ſu
ta	te	ti	to	tu

Page 1

va	ve	vi	vo	
wa	we	we	wo	
ya	ye	yi	yo	
za	ze	zi	zo	zu
ab	eb	ib	ob	ub
ac	ec	ic	uc	uc
ad	ed	id	od	ud
af	ef	if	of	uf
ag	eg	ig	og	ug
ak	ek	ik	ok	uk
al	el	il	ol	ul
am	em	im	om	um
an	en	in	on	un
ap	ep	ip	op	up
ar	er	ir	or	ur
as	es	is	os	us
at	et	it	ot	ut
ax	ex	ix	ox	ux
bla	ble	bli	blo	blu

A 2

Page 2

bra	bre	bri	bro	bru
cha	che	chi	cho	chu
cla	cle	cli	clo	clu
dra	dre	dri	dro	dru
fra	fre	fri	fro	fru
gla	gle	gli	glo	glu
han	hen	hin	hon	hun
kna	kne	kni	kno	knu
lad	led	lid	lod	lud
man	men	min	mon	mun
nap	nep	nip	nop	nup
one	old	ore	out	ous
pan	pen	pin	pon	pun
qua	que	qui	quo	quu
ran	ren	rin	ron	run
fam	fem	fim	fom	fum
tra	tre	tri	tro	tru
van	ven	vin	von	vun
and	art	are	ale	ape
bad	bed	bid	bit	bin

Page 3

cat	cap	car	can	cob
bag	cag	fag	nag	rag
beg	leg	big	dig	fig
pig	wig	bog	fog	hog
bug	dug	mug	rug	lug
ham	ram	dim	him	rim
gum	hum	rum	fum	tum
ben	den	hen	pen	ten
din	kin	gin	pin	fin
con	fon	ton	hon	von
bun	gun	nun	pun	run
cap	gap	lap	map	tap
dip	hip	lip	nip	rip
fop	hop	lop	mop	fop
bar	far	mar	tar	war
bat	cat	fat	hat	rat
bet	get	let	met	net
bit	fit	hit	nit	pit
dot	got	hot	lot	not

A 3

Page 4

but	cut	hut	nut	rut
rex	fex	vex	fix	fix
box	fox	the	for	out
cry	dry	fly	thy	try

The Sun is up my Boy,
Get out of thy Bed,
Go thy way for the Cow,
Let her eat the Hay.
Now the Sun is fet,
And the Cow is put up,
The Boy may go to his Bed.
Go not in the Way of a bad Man;
Do not tell a Lie my Son.

blab	crab	ftab	fwab	ft	fh
chub	club	grub	fnub	ff	ffi
bred	bled	fled	fhed	ff	ffl
brag	drag	flag	fnag	fi	fh
brim	grim	fwim	trim	fi	ct
crum	drum	plum	fcum	fl	&
bran	clan	plan	fpan	fl	

Page 5

hin	grin	fhin	thin
hap	clap	trap	fnap
hip	clip	fhip	trip
hop	crop	drop	fhop
ace	lace	mace	race
nice	nice	rice	vice
jade	jade	made	wade
hide	ride	fide	tide
tage	page	rage	fage
bake	cake	make	rake
bale	dale	gale	male
pale	fale	tale	vale
bile	file	mile	pile
hole	mole	pole	role
mule	rule	came	dame
lame	game	lame	name
ime	time	come	fome
bane	lane	mane	pane
dine	fine	kine	line
pine	wine	bone	hon

Page 6

back	lack	pack	fack
deck	neck	peck	reck
kick	lick	nick	fick
dock	lock	mock	rock
cold	fold	gold	hold
balk	talk	walk	filk
call	fall	gall	wall
bell	fell	fell	tell
fill	hill	kill	mill
halt	malt	falt	part
belt	felt	melt	pelt
damp	lamp	ramp	vamp
pump	lump	jump	rump
band	hand	land	fand
bend	fend	lend	mend
bind	find	kind	mind
bond	fond	pond	long
king	ring	fing	wing

The Dove doth no harm,
The Lamb doth no harm,

Page 7

A good boy doth no harm.
The Eye of the Lord is on them that fear him. He will love them, and do them good.
He will keep their Feet in the Way they go, and fave them from the Paths of Death.

ab-fence	ar-rant	bot-tom
a corn	art ift	bri dle
ac tor	bar ber	bro ther
ad der	bar rel	bow els
ad vent	bet ter	car rot
af ter	bit ter	car-ter
al fo	bor der	cam el
am ber	bo fom	can dle
an gel	bri-er	cap tain
a ny	bro ken	cap tive
art ful	bru tifh	car goe
art lefs	bra zen	com fort
ar dent	bod kin	com mon

Page 8

com-mit	dra-per	en-ter
com pile	drug get	e vent
com pofe	drunk ard	ev il
com pute	du ty	ex alt
con cord	ear ly	ex act
con dole	ear neft	ex port
con vert	ea fy	ex pound
dal ly	ed dy	fac tor
dam fel	ef fect	fag got
dam fon	ef fort	fal low
dan ger	el bow	falf ly
dark ly	el der	fa mine
dar ling	e lect	fan cy
de bafe	em bark	farm er
de bate	em pire	fa tal
de fend	en camp	fa ther
de fraud	en dow	fat nefs
de lay	en gine	fear ful
din ner	en joy	fea ther

Page 9

fea-ture	ha-bit	im-pair
fel low	hack ney	im pale
fe male	hal ter	im pend
fen nel	ham mer	im plant
gal lon	han dle	im ply
gal lop	hap pen	im prefs
gam mon	har den	im print
gan der	har dy	in fant
gar land	har lot	in vite
gar lick	har veft	in ward
gar ment	hel met	joy ful
gar ret	her mit	jour nal
gar ter	hun gry	kind nefs
gen tle	huf band	king dom
gin ger	hun ter	kinf man
glim mer	hur ry	lad der
glit ter	i dle	la ment
gun ner	i dol	lan tern
gut ter	i mage	lap wing
gui nea	im prove	lat chet

Page 10

late-ly	mal-let	mar-tyr
law ful	man kind	mo ment
law yer	man ner	mor tal
lim ber	man tle	mar vel
li mit	ma nure	ma fon
lin tel	mar ket	mar fhal
lof ty	mar row	
ma lice	mar-ry	

The Lark will fly in the Field,
The Cat doth run after the Moufe,
The Chub fwims in the Brook,
And the good Boy will love to do
good in his place.

na-tive	ne-ver	nur-ture
na ture	new nefs	o bey
nap kin	no ble	ob ject
nar row	no tice	ob tain
need ful	num ber	of fend
net tle	nut meg	op prefs
	A 6	

Page 11

or-der	quar-rel	re-cord
pad dle	quar ry	re fuge
pad lock	quar ter	re fufe
pain ful	quick en	rem nant
pa late	quick ly	re ward
pam per	qui et	re tail
pa per	qui ver	rich es
par cel	rab bet	rid dle
par ty	rack et	ri ver
pa rent	raf ter	rob ber
part ed	rai ment	rot ten
part ing	rain bow	fab bath
pil grim	ran fom	fad dle
pon der	ra for	fad nefs
pro fefs	ra ven	fad ly
pro tect	rea dy	faf fron
pro verb	rai fon	fai lor
pul let	reap er	fcho lar
pur ple	rea fon	fe cret
pur pofe	re bel	fel dom

Page 12

Page 13

The Cow gives us Milk,
The Sheep fpares us Wool,
The Hen lays Eggs,
The good Boy and the good Girl learn their Books.
Good Boys do well.
Bad Boys go to Ruin.

fer-pent	flum-ber	ten-der
fe date	fo lid	thank ful
fer vant	for ry	thun der
fer vice	fted faft	time ly
fha dow	fter ling	tim ber
fhil ling	ftew ard	tor ment
fhort ly	fuf fer	to tal
fick nefs	fu gar	tra der
fig net	fwift ly	tri al
fil ver	fwol len	trump et
fim ple	tem per	tu mult
fix ty	tem peft	tun nage

Page 13

Page 14

tun-nel	un-to	weft-ward
tur key	ut-ter	wet fhod
tur nip	ufe ful	whif per
turn er	up per	wil ful
tu tor	up fhot	will ing
va cant	up fide	win ter
var nifh	ut moft	wif dom
vel vet	wa fer	wor fhip
ven ture	wake ful	wor fted
vef fel	wan der	wor thy
vin tage	wan ton	yon der
vint ner	war rant	youth ful
vi per	wel fare	
vir gin	wed ding	
un der	weft ern	

The Rain makes the Grafs grow,
The Air is of great Ufe to us,
The Sun does us good,
It is the Lord who fends us all good Things. O my Child love the Lord,

Page 14

Page 15

and ftrive to be good, that it may be well with thee when thou dies; For when a good Child dies, his Soul goes to Chrift above, and lives in Joy for ever and ever: But when one that is wicked dies in his Sins, his Soul finds no Reft in the other World.

Walk therefore my Son in the good Way, fo fhall thy laft End be Peace.

ab-fo-lute	bla-ma-ble
ac ti on	but ter fly
af ter ward	ca ni fter
al ma nack	ca pa ble
al pha bet	car pen ter
a ni mal	car ri age
ap pe tite	car ri er
be ne fit	cau ti ous
bit ter nefs	ce le brate
be wil der	cer tain ly

A 8

Page 15

Page 16

cer-ti-fy	ex-er-cife
com pa ny	fac to ry
clo thi er	fa cul ty
con fi dent	faith ful ly
con tra ry	fal fi fy
cu ri ous	fa mi ly
de fo late	fa ther lefs
di a mond	fa vor ite .
dig ni fy	fi nal ly
dif fer ence	fi nifh er
dif fer ent	fir ma ment
di li gent	fol low er
du ra ble	for ci ble
du ti ful	for mer ly
eat a ble	for ti tude
e ne my	for tu nate
en mi ty	fu ri ous
e ven ing	ge ne ral
e ve ry	gen tle man
e vi dent	glo ri fy

Page 16

glo-ri-ous   hy-po-crite
glut to ny   ig no rance
go vern or   im pi ous
gra ci ous   im pu dent
gra du al   in di gence
gra vi ty   in di go
gra zi er   in do lent
gree di ly   in fa my
grid i ron   in fan cy
guar di an   in fi del
hap pi nefs   in ju ry
har mo ny   in no cence
heart i ly   in ftru ment
hea ven ly   in ti mate
hea vi nefs   in wardly
hi fto ry   i vo ry
hi ther to   ju ni per
hor ri bly   ju fti fy
ho fpi tal   kna ve ry
hu mor fome   la ti tude

Page 17

la-ven-der   mef-fen-ger
le ga cy   migh ti ly
li a ble   mil li on
li be ral   mi ni ftry
li ber ty   mi ra cle
lot te ry   mi fe ry
low er moft   mock e ry
lu fti ly   mo nu ment
mag ni fy   mov a ble
ma je fty   mul ber ry
ma la dy   mul ti tude
ma ni fold   na ti on
man ner ly   na tu ral
ma ri gold   no ta bly
mar ri age   nu me ral
mar tyr dom   nur fe ry
me di tate   ob li gate
me mo ry   ob fti nate
mer ci ful   ob vi ate
mer ci lefs   oc cu py

Page 18

The Lord is good to them that wait for him, to the Soul that feek-eth him.

It is good that a Man both hope and qui-et-ly wait, for the Help of the Lord.

It is good for a Man that he bear the Yoke in his Youth.

He fit-teth a-lone, and keep-eth Silence, becaufe he hath born it upon him.

He put-teth his Mouth in the Duft if fo be there may be Hope.

of-fer-ing   pa-ren-tage
o ni on   paf fen ger
o pe rate   paf fi on
or der ly   pa ti ent
o ri gin   pa tri arch
or na ment   pe ri od
pa ra ble   pi e ty

Page 19

pi-ti-ful   re-fi-due
plen ti ful   re fo lute
po ver ty   re ve rence
pow er ful   ri ot ous
pre fent ly   rob be ry
pro di gal   fa tis fy
pub li can   fanc ti fy
qua li ty   fe cond ly
quan ti ty   fen fi ble
quar rel fome   fen ti ment
quar ter ly   fe pa rate
ra ri ty   fe ri ous
ra ti fy   fet tle ment
rea di ly   fe ven ty
rec kon ing   fix ti eth
re com pence   fla ve ry
re gu lar   flip pe ry
re gu late   fo lemn ly
re me dy   fol di er
re pro bate   fo li tude

Page 20

for-row-ful	ve-ni-fon
fo ve reign	vic to ry
fpec ta cle	vi ne gar
ftur ge on	vi o lence
teach a ble	vir tu ous
te di ous	vi fit or
tem per ate	un der hand
tem po ral	un der moft
te ne ment	u ni form
ter ri ble	ufe ful nefs
ter ri fy	ut ter ly
te fta ment	war ri or
te fti fy	wea ri ed
to ward ly	wea ri fome
tra vel ler	wick ed nefs
trou ble fome	wil der nefs
trump et er	won der ful
ty ran ny	
va li ant	
va ni ty	

Page 21

Blefs-ed are the pure in the Way, who walk in the Law of the Lord.

Blefs-ed are they that keep his Law, and that feek him with all their Heart.

The Lord is an-gry with the Proud, and with them who turn a-fide to Lies.

The Earth is full of the Good-nefs of the Lord. O that all Men would love him and o-bey him.

con-di-ti-on	di-ver-fi-ty
con fef fi on	di vi fi on
con ten ti on	e lec ti on
con ver fi on	e nor mi ty
cor rec ti on	e qua li ty
cre a ti on	e ter ni ty
de fec ti on	ex pe di ent
de ri fi on	ex po fi tor
de vo ti on	ex e cu tor
dex te ri ty	foun da ti on
di rec ti on	fru gal i ty

Page 22

fu-tu-ri-ty	per-pe-tu-al
har mo ni ous	no mi na ti on
hu ma nity	ob li ga ti on
i do la ter	pre pa ra ti on
im me di ate	re fo lu ti on
im pe ni tent	re pu ta ti on
im pu ri ty	re for ma ti on
in fec ti on	
in firm i ty	
in i qui ty	One	1	I
in ven ti on	two	2	II
me lo di ous	three	3	III
me mo ri al	four	4	IV
mi nor i ty	five	5	V
mo ral i ty	fix	6	VI
mor tal i ty	fe-ven	7	VII
na ti vi ty	eight	8	VIII
o be di ent	nine	9	IX
o pi ni on	ten	10	X
per fec ti on	eleven	11	XI
	twelve	12	XII

Page 23

There was a certain rich Man which was cloth-ed in Purple and fine Lin-en, and far-ed fump-tu-oufly e-ve-ry Day.

And there was a cer-tain Beg-gar nam-ed La-za-rus, which was laid at his Gate, full of Sores.

And de-fir-ing to be fed with the Crumbs which fell from the rich Man's Ta-ble : More-over the Dogs came and lick-ed his Sores.

And it came to pafs that the Beg-gar di-ed, and was car-ri-ed by the An-gels in-to A-bra-ham's Bo-fom, the rich Man al-fo di-ed, and was bu-ri-ed.

And in Hell he lift up his Eyes, be-ing in Tor-ments, and fe-eth A-bra-ham a-far off and La-za-rus in his Bo-fom.

Page 24

And he cri-ed, and faid, Fa-ther
A-bra-ham, have Mer-cy on me, and
fend La-za-rus, that he may dip the
Tip of his Fin-ger in Wa-ter, and
cool my Tongue, for I am tor-ment-ed
in this Flame.

But A-bra-ham faid, Son, re-mem-
ber that thou in thy Life time receiv-
edft thy good Things, and like-wife
La-za-rus e-vil Things, but now he is
com-fort-ed, and thou art tor-ment-ed.

And be-fide all this, be-tween us and
you there is a Gulf fix-ed, fo that they
which would pafs from hence to you
can-not; nei-ther can they pafs to us,
that would come from thence.

Then he faid, I pray thee, there-fore,
Fa-ther, that thou would-eft fend him
to my Fa-ther's Houfe.

For I have five Bre-thren, that he

Page 25

may te-fti-fy un-to them, left they al-fo
come in-to this Place of Tor-ment.

A-bra-ham faid un-to him, they have
Mo-fes and the Pro-phets; let them
hear them.

And he faid; nay, Fa-ther A-bra-
ham, but if one went un-to them from
the Dead, they will re-pent.

And he faid un-to him, if they hear
not Mo-fes and the Pro-phets, nei-ther
will they be per-fuad-ed though one
rofe from the Dead.

Re-mem-ber now thy Cre-a-tor in the
Days of thy Youth, while the e-vil
Days come not, and the Years draw
nigh, when thou fhalt fay, I have no
Plea-fure in them.

In all thy Ways ac-know-ledge him,
and he fhall di-rect thy Paths.

Page 26

Keep thy Heart with all Di-li-gence,
for out of it are the If-fues of Life.

My Son, keep my Words, and lay
up my Com-mand-ments with thee.

Fear God, and keep his Com-mand-
ments, for this is the whole Du-ty of
Man.

What does it pro-fit a Man if he
gain the whole World, and lofe his
own Soul? Or what fhall a Man give
in Ex-change for his Soul?

Let your Light fo fhine be-fore
Men, that they may fee your good
Works, and glo-ri-fy your Fa-ther
which is in Hea-ven.

Thou fhalt love the Lord thy God
with all thy Soul, and with all thy
Strength, and with all thy Mind.

Take good heed, there-fore un-to
your-felves, that ye love the Lord your
God.

Page 27

Love not the World, nei-ther the
Things that are in the World: If a-ny
Man love the World, the Love of the
Fa-ther is not in him.

For all that is in the World, the
Luft of the Flefh, the Luft of the Eye,
and the Pride of Life, is not of the Father, but of the World.

And the World paff-eth a-way, and
the Luft there-of; but he that doth
the Will of God, a-bid-eth for e-ver.

Make me to know my End, and the
Mea-fure of my Days, what it is; that
I may know how frail I am.

O how great is the Good-nefs, which
thou haft laid up for them that fear
thee, and which thou haft wrought for
them that truft in thee, e-ven be-fore
the Sons of Men.

Yea, though I walk through the Val-

Page 28

ley of the Sha-dow of Death, I will fear no E-vil, for thou art with me, thy Rod and thy Staff they com-fort me.

Be ye fol-low-ers of them who through Faith and Pa-ti-ence in-he rit the Pro-mi-fes

God is our Re-fuge and Strength, there-fore will I not fear, though the Earth be re-mov-ed. Be-caufe we truft in the liv-ing God, we fhall not be a-fraid of e-vil Ti-dings, but in Qui-et-nefs, and in Con-fi-dence fhall be our Strength ; may they fay who faith-ful-ly fol-low Chrift.

Behold a certain Lawyer ftood up, and tempted our bleffed Saviour, fay-ing, Mafter, what fhall I do to inhe-rit eternal Life ?

He faid unto him, what is written

Page 29

in the Law ? how readeft thou ?

And he anfwering, faid, Thou fhalt love the Lord thy God with all thy Heart, and with all thy Soul, and with all thy Strength, and with all thy mind ; and thy neighbour as thy felf.

And he faid unto him, Thou haft an-fwered right, this do, and thou fhaltlive.

But he, willing to juftify himfelf, faid unto Jefus, and who is my neighbour ?

And Jefus anfwering, faid, A certain Man went down from Jerufalem, to Jeri-co, and fell among Thieves, which ftrip-ped him of his Raiment, and wounded him, and departed, leaving him half-dead

And it fell out there came down a cer-tain Prieft that Way ; and when he faw him he paffed by on the other Side.

And likewife a Levite when he was at the Place came and looked on him, and paffed by on the other Side.

Page 30

But a certain Samaritan, as he jour-neyed, came where he was ; and when he faw him, he had compaffion on him,

And went to him, and bound up his wounds, pouring in Oil and Wine, and fet him on his own Beaft and brought him to an Inn, and took Care of him.

And on the Morrow when he departed he took out two Pence, and gave them to the Hoft, and faid unto him, Take care of him, and whatfoever thou fpend-eft more, when I come again, I will re-pay thee.

Which now of thefe three thinkeft thou, was the Neighbour to him that fell among the Thieves.

And he faid, he that fhewed Mercy upon him. Then faid Jefus unto him Go and do thou likewife.

Page 31

Related Writings by Contemporaries

This part of the Source Book *contains writings from Woolman's time, providing points of comparison, or shedding some light on Woolman himself: (1) selections from Mercy Redman's "Journal"; (2) an account of the visit of the Delawares to Philadelphia in 1760, probably by Anthony Benezet, "Some Account of the Behaviour and Sentiments of a Number of Well-Disposed Indians..." and (3) a collection of letters written by a fellow passenger on the voyage to England, and by Friends in England who were struck by Woolman's "singular" appearance and by him as a person.*

Mercy Redman (1721–1778) was a recorded minister as was Woolman. She along with others traveled for a while with Woolman on his journey in 1760 to the New England Yearly Meeting in Newport, Rhode Island. The manuscript of her journal is less polished than Woolman's Journal. *Reading her account of the same journey, one gains an appreciation for the literary achievement of Woolman's* Journal. *Mercy Redman, however, gives us another perspective on the life of travelling ministers and the quality of Quaker worship as she observed it. In a different way, she provides us with a record, in some detail, of the perseverance and commitment of Quakers travelling in the ministry (on this journey she reports having visited "eighty-seven meetings"!), the joint effort of the ministers working and travelling together, and the difficulties at meetings for worship in which Mercy Redman often found the sensitivity to the spirit less than satisfactory ("... a dull lifeless time it was. We had something to say to them, but all did not seem to raise the dead"). She leaves a record of appreciation felt by others for John Woolman's presence.*

In some bibliographic references, Woolman is described as the author of "Some Account of the Behaviour and Sentiments of a Number of Well-Disposed Indians." However, since a work with the same title is listed among works of Anthony Benezet (1713–1784), it seems probable that Benezet was the author, and that he was also at the meeting in Philadelphia in 1760 that Woolman describes in, "The Substance of Some Conversation with Paponahoal the Indian Chief..." printed in the Other Writings section of the Source Book.

Benezet was a close friend of Woolman and shared many of his concerns. Of French Huguenot background, he fled with his family after the revocation of the Edict of Nantes, spent some time in the Netherlands before going on to England, where he became associated with Friends. In his late teens, he migrated to America and became a member of the Burlington Meeting to which Woolman also belonged. He taught school for many years, set up a school for girls, and later opened a school in his home for the children of former slaves. In addition to the concerns shared with Woolman, he was concerned for the Acadians, some of whom had come to Philadelphia after their eviction from Canada. He wrote extensively on a number of issues, and carried on correspondence with people outside the Society of Friends, including Benjamin Franklin and European rulers. He was much concerned with slavery, and he was interested in the Indians. He did not visit them in the wilderness, as Woolman did, but he was at the second meeting with them at Easton, PA, which he describes in another report, and he continued to work with them after they were moved from Wyalusing and interned in Philadelphia.

"Some Account..." is quite detailed. It reinforces the impression from Woolman of the religious experience of Papunehang, his vision quest, his pacifism, and his appreciation of Friends. It also explains perhaps, even more fully, why Woolman was apparently not interested in converting the Indians.

There are no authentic portraits of John Woolman, but there are accounts of his appearance and his effect on other people. The selections called "As Others Saw Woolman (Letters from the Journey to England)" include three letters by Samuel Emlen, who was a younger Friend, and fellow minister. The fourth letter, from John Pemberton, is clearly intended to smooth Woolman's way in England. Pemberton was a close friend of Woolman's, who accompanied him part of the way on the trip to Wyalusing. The Pembertons were prominent, wealthy Friends, and leaders of Philadelphia Yearly Meeting. The remaining selections are by British Friends. It seems clear that Woolman's white clothes set him apart from others. They attracted attention, but also offended some people. But there appears to have been great appreciation for Woolman as a person.

Mercy Redman's "Journal"[44]

The ninth of the fifth month 1760, my friend, Ann Gauntt and I set out in order to visit Friends in New England and Long Island, and that night came to Benjamin Johnson's at Toms River, and though they were not Friends the woman of the house was desirous that we should have a meeting among the neighbours, which we found freedom to assent to, and were not easy to omit; and notice being given to the near neighbours, and though the time

---

44.   Mercy Redman's spellings for most names of people and places have been preserved here.

was short, there came as many I believe as could, and we had a meeting with them, and our Master that is a present helper in every needful time, and worthy to be trusted in, was pleased to hand forth something to us suitable to the states of the people, which was both to ours and their satisfaction, and we parted in much love and affection, more than many that are called of our Society. And we set out that afternoon for Squan, in order to have a meeting among the few Friends that dwell there. And according on the next day, it being first day of the week, and 11th of the month, there gathered a pretty many people, some not being of our Society, so that the house was nearly full. And a close exercising time it was indeed because of the indifferency of the people, but the way being a little opened, we both had something to speak to them, and it ended to more satisfaction.

And went from there to the house of Thomas Tilton, it being hard by, and set out that afternoon for Shrewsbury, being accompanied by the aforesaid Tilton's son, who informed me that he had had a necessity laid upon him to go and sit in their meetinghouse alone, on the weekday, there being no meeting established at that time on the weekday, which I thought worth remarking of one who is but quite a youth, and since that the monthly meeting has granted a weekday meeting at that place.

We came that night to Joseph Wardel's at Shrewsbury, and notice being given, we had a meeting next day at their meetinghouse, it being the second day of the week, and though the people seemed to be got too much into indifferency, yet the most high was pleased to renew his visitation of love and favour to the people, and the meeting ended to good satisfaction, which I desire that they and we may gratefully remember. And went from thence that afternoon to Nathan Tilton's, it being on the way to Woodbridge, and there stayed all next day, the weather being wet, and on fourth day we rode in the rain to Woodbridge, being accompanied by several Friends, and on fifth day was at their monthly meeting, which was small, and for a while very dull, being mostly made up with elderly and middle aged people; but truth seemed to arise and make way, so that we had pretty good service and satisfaction among them, and I believe there is an honest remnant belonging to that monthly meeting. And they were advised to bring their children to meeting for discipline, that when the present generation may be removed, the succeeding generation may be favoured to come up rightly, which much depends upon the honest care of parents, which often seems attended with a blessing. And next morning we set out for York, being accompanied by Benjamin Shadwell, and crossed two ferries, one being nine miles over, and got to York a little after the middle of the day, and making but a short stay there, we travelled twenty miles that afternoon back of York to the house of Aaron Quimbee, and was accompanied by young John Burling and George Bowne, two hopeful youths. And there we stayed till first day, it being the 18th day of the month, and had a good meeting that day at West Chester among the few Friends that are there, and a pretty many other Societies, and our good Master was pleased to reach forth a hand of divine goodness and heavenly help to our comfort and strength. The people sat very quiet and the meeting ended to good satisfaction.

On second day we were at Marrineck among a few Friends, which meeting was hard and laborious, and we had painful labour under a sense of declension that seemed to appear in them parts among Friends; but the meeting ended pretty well, for which favour, with many others, I hope we may be truly thankful. And rode that afternoon about 9 miles and lodged at John Cornal's, and next day we had a meeting at the Purchase, and tho' religion in them parts seems to be at a very low ebb, the Most High was pleased to renew his visitation of love to us, and we had a comfortable meeting together and went home with Moses Quimbee; and on fourth day we had a meeting at Chappaqua, and though very dull in the beginning, yet our good Master was pleased to condescend and favour us with a good meeting, and it ended well; and we lodged that night at Moses Powel's, and on fifth day we rode about ten miles and had a meeting in a dwelling house near Compound, which was mostly made up of a shattered raw people, which looked very dull to us at the beginning, but the divine notice of the Almighty was extended and ability given beyond expectation, and the meeting ended to good satisfaction and thankfulness unto the author of all good. And went that afternoon about sixteen miles to Samuel Feals's, and there stayed till seventh day and had a meeting at his dwelling house, which was a sore exercising time. The people seemed to have but little sense of Truth, though they make a profession of it. We had some painful labour among them, which rested with some satisfaction on our minds; and rode that afternoon about seventeen miles to Oblong and lodged at Benjamin

Faris's; and on first day, which was the twenty fifth day of the month, we had a meeting at their meeting house, and though there was some things closely spoke to, yet it was a good comfortable meeting, and ended to satisfaction, which seemed like balm to our drooping spirits; and on second day we went seventeen miles to Oswego, and had a little meeting with a few Friends, and although a great part of them looked but raw, yet we was favoured with the notice of our Heavenly Master, and it was a good meeting which I thought made that saying good that the Lord looks not as man looks, and lodged that night at Lot Trips, and on third day we had a meeting at the Nine Partners, and an exercising painful time it was. The true seed seemed much oppressed, but the way a little opened, and we found ability to speak some things to them, which was to some satisfaction. And we lodged that night at Jonathan Holmes; and next day we rode twenty-five miles to New Milford to a meeting that was appointed at four o'clock that afternoon, which was very small by reason the people had not general notice, and it was not to much satisfaction.

And on fifth, sixth, and seventh day, we was employed in riding through the government of Connecticut, which was upwards of an hundred miles riding, and came on seventh day afternoon to the house of young Peter Davis's, and on the first day of the sixth month and first day of the week, we was at their meeting at Westerly with about thirty Friends, and the Lord favoured us with a good meeting among them few, which caused us with thankful hearts to acknowledge to his goodness, who is the true helper of his people. And we lodged that night at the house of Thomas Wilbur's, and had a meeting that evening in his house, with a sick woman that had very hard fits, and seemed under great affliction of body and mind. She expressed much satisfaction and relief, after the meeting was over that she received thereby. And on second day we had a meeting at Hopkinton, which seemed pretty open, and it was a comfortable meeting, and we hope serviceable; and lodged that night at Solomon Hawks's, and on third day we had a meeting at Richmantown, and a poor hard time it was, though we had some satisfaction in the discharge of our duty among them.

We went home that night with James Perry and had a meeting on fourth day at South Kingston Higher, and the Lord was pleased to exalt his truth and power over all, and it was a good meeting and ended to satisfaction, which a little revived our spirits, and we lodged that night at Peleg Peckham's, and on fifth day we had a meeting at South Kingston Lower, and a dull lifeless time it was. We had something to say to them, but all did not seem to raise the dead. These four latter meetings were in the Narraganset country, and we intended a meeting on sixth day at Conanicut, but a strong easterly storm arising, it was thought not safe for us to cross the ferry, and we stayed at Thomas Hasserd's till seventh day, and then set out for Newport on Rhode Island, and crossed two ferries, each being three miles over, and came to Newport, and stayed at Thomas Richardson's, and was at two meetings at Newport, one in the forenoon and the other in the afternoon. Both was very large, and though we went to them in great fear, yet they was both satisfactory meetings, which drew from us thankfulness unto the blessed author of all good; and in the evening we went to visit a sick man in the town and had some little service with him. On second day we had a meeting at Seconnet, which was but dull and hard, but ended with some satisfaction.

We lodged that night at Abraham Barker's, and had a meeting on third day at Tivertown, and it was we hope a profitable season to the people, and we was helped to discharge our duty among them. We crossed the ferry that evening over to Rhode Island again, and there stayed until first day and was at Pockmuth meeting, the first day of Newport Yearly Meeting being usually held at that place on fifth day; and it was a pretty good meeting, being attended by several Friends from divers parts who came on a religious visit to Friends in that country: John Storer from old England, and our worthy and ancient Friend Elizabeth Shipley from Pennsylvania, and her companion, Hannah Foster; John Woolman and his companion, Samuel Eastborn, my companion and I. And that afternoon all the aforesaid Friends went to Newport in order to be at the Yearly Meeting the next day, and we all lodged at Thomas Richardson's during our stay there, and was very kindly entertained.

The Yearly Meeting holding four days, our good Master was pleased to remember us and to favour us with the shedding abroad of his love to the uniting us in a near manner to himself and one to another; and I hope it was a good time to some of the youth, there being a tender remnant among them of the younger sort. For all those favours with many more I hope we shall not be forgetful. Our Friend John Storer was very much employed in rectifying their discipline, things being much out of right regulation among them, so that he omitted attending several of our meetings of worship, it being his business to visit meetings for discipline this second time of his coming into these parts.

And after the conclusion of the Yearly Meeting, we went to James Michel's, in order for visiting the meetings in Dartmouth, and on the third day of the week we went to visit a young family of Friends and had good satisfaction. They were tender young people. On fourth day we had a meeting at Acohesett in which we had hard work, though we was helped to discharge our duty, John Woolman and Samuel Eastborn being in company with us all that week. And on fifth day, we and the aforesaid Friends had a meeting at Newtown, which was a satisfactory meeting, and in the afternoon we went to visit a sick Friend, the wife of Abraham Tucker, and had a good season with her, and lodged that night at Joseph Tucker's, and had a setting in his family in the evening, and I hope we had good service among his children.

And of sixth day we had a meeting at Aquishart and a hard time it was from beginning to ending. And that night we lodged at Nathan Davis's, the son of our worthy Friend Nicholas Davis, and on seventh day we had a meeting at Long Plain, which was but a low time; and on the fifth day of the week and twenty-second of the month, John Woolman and Samuel Eastborn went to Rochester meeting, and we was at Poniganset, John Storer likewise being there. The meeting was very large and likewise very hard, the people being got greatly into stupidity and hard heartedness: it was thought there was upwards of a thousand people at that meeting. We was at their monthly meeting on second day at the same place, John Storer, John Woolman and Samuel, and Comfort Hoag from eastward, all being at the monthly meeting, which was very large, and the meeting for worship pretty well. But the meeting of discipline was filled up with a great number of young people, not members, that rendered it very burdensome to us that were strangers to the place, and likewise to that custom; and it was much advised against, by both men and women; and the men drew a minute and sent to the women, in order to strengthen them in bearing a hand against that practice.

We lodged that night at Jonathan Hussey's, and next day we and John Woolman, Samuel Eastborn, William Lightfoot from Philadelphia, and

Comfort Hoag and her companion, with a pretty many other Friends went on board a vessel for the Island of Nantucket; and having but little wind we was obliged to go ashore at a place called Tarpolian Cove in the evening, and there we stayed in a tavern that night, and next morning at four o'clock we went on board again, and was all day in the vessel; and in the evening twelve of us got in the boat that belonged to the vessel and rowed to shore. We got to the town about eight o'clock that evening and lodged at Sarah Barney's. Some Friends in town took a boat and brought the other Friends onshore that we left in the vessel. It being low water the vessel could not come within six miles of the town. It was called 60 miles by water. On fifth day we had no meeting but spent the day in visiting some Friends.

On sixth day the Yearly Meeting came on, and a hard meeting we had, though my companion was favoured to discharge her duty honestly and speak to the states of the people. There appears a great declension among the people, though I believe there is an honest hearted remnant among them. In the afternoon we rode two miles out of town to visit a sick and aged Friend, the son of Mary Starbuck that our Friend John Richardson gives an account of in his Journal. I believe he is a good old man; he is aged about eighty-eight years. We had good satisfaction in the visit, and was accompanied by William Lightfoot and several other Friends, and in the evening we had a little setting at Sarah Barney's, with a few Friends that came in of seventh day which was the second day of the Yearly Meeting. The Lord favoured us with a good and comfortable meeting, and likewise the select meeting in the morning was pretty well, considering the times.

In the afternoon our aforesaid men Friends appointed a meeting among the Indians of that place. There was a pretty many of them met, and the Friends had good satisfaction in the visit; the Indians was still and attentive.

We spent the afternoon in visiting sick Friends, to good satisfaction, which paid us for our labour richly. The twenty-ninth of the month and the first day of the week, we was at two meetings at the meeting house, it being the third day of the Yearly Meeting, which was large and both pretty solid, though close doctrine to deliver.

In the evening we had a setting in Silvenus Hussey's family. Our Friend John Woolman had some solid and seasonable advice to the few Friends present. On second day their monthly meeting came on and select meeting in the morning. They was both good solid meetings and Truth seemed to be exalted over all its enemies, which gave us new life. The meeting of business was also solid, and some good advice given. Our Friend John Woolman came in among the women, and was directed to drop some very seasonable advice to mothers of children concerning their educating of them. In the evening we had a setting at Sarah Barney's with a few Friends, which was satisfactory, John Woolman being with us. There seems to be great openness and tenderness in the minds of some Friends in that place. I desire that remnants may be favoured to keep their place rightly, and may grow in experience that they may come to be helpful to others that the breaches may be repaired.

On third day morning at two o'clock in the morning we arose and went on board the vessel with our former passengers, with a few more added, in order to go to Woods Hole, but the wind being quite contrary, we presently went on shore again, and returning to our lodging, went to bed again, and when we arose, the wind not yet suiting, we found freedom to appoint another meeting, to which came a pretty many people, and it seemed a favourable time. My companion was drawn forth largely to speak to the state of the people. On fourth day morning at two o'clock we was called to go on board again, the wind being fair. We set sail and got ashore at seven o'clock in the evening at Woods Hole. I was exceeding seasick, and several other of the passengers, which made it seem very tedious. I did not recover it for several days, which caused travelling to be very wearisome. This last water voyage I think this was called fifteen leagues. We lodged at Steven Boardman's, about 5 miles from Woods Hole.

On the third day of the seventh month and fifth of the week, we had a meeting at Falmouth, which was a very dull time to us, and I believe to the people also. We lodged that night at Joshua Wing's, John Woolman and Samuel being still with us. We went the next day, the sixth of the week to Sandige monthly meeting. William Lightfoot took cold on the water which rendered him unable to travel, and we was obliged to leave him at Steven Boardman's, and next day he met us at Sandige, and was pretty well recruited. The monthly meeting aforesaid was but small and likewise but dull. A great coolness and indifferency appears among many of the professors of Truth in them parts, though I hope there is a remnant that desires to do well. On seventh day was their quarterly meeting at the same place. We was all at it and it was a good meeting and ended well for which favour I was thankful.

That afternoon my companion and Samuel Eastborn set out with several other Friends in order to be at Yarmouth meeting on first day, which was about seventeen miles from Sandige. John Woolman and I stayed at Sandige's first day meeting, which I hope was a profitable season to the people. In the afternoon we had a setting with Daniel Allen's family; I think it was a pretty good time. In the evening my companion and Samuel returned from Yarmouth, and on second day morning we all took leave of our kind Friend Joshua Wings and his wife, who was very kind to us. We made our home with them all the time we were at Sandige; and went that day to Nathan Davis's, in order to have a meeting on third day at Rochester.

John and Samuel parted with us on second day and went for Rhode Island quarterly meeting, and we visited the meetings about Dartmouth. The meeting at Rochester was hard and laborious, though we was helped to labour faithfully among them. On fourth day we had a meeting at Poniganset, and there was likewise a marriage, and a painful time it was because of the many dry professors, but we was favoured to clear our minds among them. We lodged on third day night at Joseph Smith's and on fourth day in the afternoon we set out toward Freetown and lodged at Gideon Allen's, and on sixth day we had a meeting at Freetown. We had very hard work in them meetings. At Dartmouth there seems a great degeneracy among the many professors of Truth in them parts. We lodged at Edward Shoves's, and had an opportunity in his family in the evening, to good satisfaction. And on sixth day we had a meeting at Tanton, and such a meeting I think I never was at before, nor never desire to be at such another. I did not think there was a sensible Friend among them.

We lodged that night at Henry Bower's. He had lately buried his wife, which seemed a very great stroke to him. We had an opportunity with him and his little ones in the morning to good satisfaction. On seventh day we had a meeting at Swansey, which was a low time, and to no great satisfaction. We rode twenty miles that afternoon, and crossed two ferries, and came to James Michel's that night, and on the first day of the week and twelfth of the month, my companion went to Poachmuth meeting, and

I was at Newport meeting in the forenoon, and in the afternoon we was both at Newport meeting, and I hope they was both pretty good meetings. On second day we had a meeting at Connanicot, being accompanied by a pretty many Friends from Newport. This latter meeting was but a hard time. After meeting we took leave of our Friends and set out for Long Island, and lodged that night at Peleg Peckham's.

On third day morning William Lightfoot met us in order to bear us company through Long Island, and several other Friends being with us, we rode thirty-six miles that day, and came to Groton that evening and lodged that night in a tavern. Next morning at seven o'clock we went on board a ferry boat, and went according to account forty miles by water, and landed on Long Island about twelve o'clock. William Lightfoot and we rode twenty-seven miles, and came to the head of the river that evening and lodged at a tavern. On fifth day morning we set out again towards Setocket, and rode twenty-seven miles and lodged at John Hallock's and had a meeting in his house on sixth day among a few Friends that dwells there abouts, which was to pretty good satisfaction. That afternoon we rode nineteen miles and lodged at the Widow Willet's, and had a meeting on seventh day at Secotog, which was but a dull time. That afternoon we went to Bethpage and lodged there, and on first day we was at their halfyear's meeting, which was large and I think a good meeting, and lodged that night at Samuel Willes's; and second day we rested, and on third day we had a meeting at Matinicock, which seemed an open time, and lodged at Isaac Dotes.

On fourth day we was at Westbury meeting, which was large, considering harvest time, and a good opportunity I think it was. We lodged that night at the Widow Litos's, and on fifth day we had a meeting at Cowneck, which seemed very dull in the beginning, though after a time the cloud seemed a little removed, and I had some service among them to my satisfaction. My companion was silent in that meeting. We lodged that night at Matthew Franklin's. On sixth day we had a meeting at Flushing, which seemed hard and laborious in the beginning, but our good Master was pleased to favour us with his heavenly help, and I think the meeting ended well which was cause of thankfulness. We lodged that night at John Way's. On seventh day we had a meeting at Newtown, which was very small; my companion had some good service among them.

We went to York that afternoon and lodged at Margaret Bowne's. On the twenty-seventh of the month and first day of the week we was at two meetings at York. Both I hope was profitable meetings. I think there was a concerned remnant in that city. On second day we crossed the ferry and got to Joseph Shadwell's that night. On third day we rode to Stony Brook, and lodged at James Olden's; on fourth day we came to Crosswicks, and there my companion and I took leave of each other in much love and affection, she intending homewards. Next day William Lightfoot and I came to Burlington and lodged that night at Daniel Smith's and set out next day in the rain, and reached home about two o'clock in the afternoon, and was received joyfully by my dear husband and children and friends, and found all well, and a good deal of peace and sweetness in my own mind, for which favours and blessings, I hope I shall gratefully live under a humble sense of. In this journey I was at eighty-seven meetings.

"Some Account Of The Behaviour And Sentiments Of A Number Of Well Disposed Indians"[45]

About the beginning of the 7th month 1760 some Indians came to Philadelphia from an Indian town called Mahachloosing situate on a branch of the Susquahanna about 200 miles from this city. Their principal business was to pay a visit to Friends, who, they understood, had sent them an invitation to come down; which apprehension of theirs was barely owing to that upon hearing some Indians were religiously disposed and refused to join the other Indians in the war, some Friend or Friends might say we should be glad to

45. The account printed in this section follows the Swarthmore College manuscript, thought to be copied from an earlier manuscript. In the Swarthmore version, the spelling of the Indian chief's name is rendered uniformly as Papoonahoal, and an extra paragraph based on later conversations is appended. For more on the purposes of Woolman's visit to Papunehang's tribe, described in *Journal* chapter 8, and the simultaneous visit of a Moravian missionary, David Zeisberger, whom Woolman mentions but does not name, see Ralph Pickett's "A Religious Encounter: John Woolman and David Zeisberger," *Quaker History* 79 (Fall 1990): 77-92. Zeisberger knew the Delaware language, was intent on conversion, and according to Pickett, baptized Papunehang shortly after Woolman left.

see them, which being repeated to them was the occasion of their visit. Yet they thought it their duty to wait upon the governor, as well to manifest their respect as to deliver three prisoners which they had redeemed from other Indians who had taken them captives, and some horses, which they had brought with them.

A time was appointed for the governor to confer with them, and a conference was held in the council chamber, the most material part of which was as follows:

Papoonahoal the Indian Chief, or as the Indians style him their minister, spoke to the following effect viz.—"That Tedeuscung called at their town on his way to Assintzing and had held council with them, and had applied for their assistance in a matter which he had much at heart, which was the redemption of the prisoners which were still captive amongst the Indians; that they had willingly complied with this request, as far as within their power, by giving them up the three only prisoners which were amongst them which they had brought with them and had delivered to the governor."

And by a string of wampum he further declared, "That now they had delivered all the captives that were in the hands of those Indians which belonged to their society or town," for, says he, "we desire to do justice and love God, and wish it was in our power to assist so that all the prisoners which were scattered in the woods every where might be brought back."

By another string he spoke again: "Brother, I am well pleased to hear of that good peace that is so well established. I heartily join in it, and desire to live in peace. Hearken, Brother: I pray you would have some pity on us, and let us have no strong liquor at all here, all we that live in the place called Mahachloosing. And if any of our young men come down, ask them where they come from, and when they say they come from Mahachaloosing, I pray you not to give them a drop of liquor, and hope you will hear us.

"Brother though we are poor we want no recompense for the prisoners or for the horses; we do not return them to you from a desire of gain. You are welcome to them, and we are glad of the opportunity of obliging you."

The governor returned them a kind answer, and told them he had prepared a few things for them, and desired their acceptance of them, upon which Papoonahoal spoke again:

"Brother—I do not come here to do any public business with the government; I am not in that character; I came on a religious account, on an invitation sent me by some religious people about twelve months ago. Therefore it frightens me to hear what you have just now spoken, viz., that you have provided some goods for me and mean to make us a present of them. I thank you for your good will, but I cannot allow myself to take them, since this would look as if I was come, as other great ones do, to receive presents. No Brother, I am perfectly satisfied with the many good things I have heard in the religious conferences that I have held, since we came here, with the Quakers. Brother, I will tell you the reason why I say I am frightened: should I lay my hands on your presents it would raise a jealousy in the breasts of those round about me, who transact the public business, and are wont to receive presents on such occasions. It would moreover be apt to corrupt my own mind and make me proud; and others would think I wanted to be a great man, which is not the case. I think on God who made us. I want to be instructed in his service and worship. I am a great lover of peace, and have never been concerned in war affairs: I have a sincere remembrance of the old friendship which subsisted between the Indians and your forefathers, and shall always observe it. I love my Brethren, the English, and they shall ever find me faithful. I was invited to come and for these reasons did come, and not to receive presents which spoil and corrupt the receivers of them. Many have misbehaved after they have received them, and many, I am afraid, came only to receive them."

Papoonahoal then complained of some abuses in trade, and said, "That they had not received the price for skins that had been promised them; that this put their young men about playing unfair tricks with the skins, by leaving on them several parts which were of no use, as the ears, paws & c. This, he added, is not as it ought to be. We should not skin our skins in such a way; but our corrupt hearts have found out this way of dealing. Brother, you see there is no love nor honesty on either side; you do wrong in altering your prices and the Indians do wrong in bringing you skins with so much badness on them. Therefore, Brother, I propose to fling this entirely away; for if it remains we shall never agree and love one another as we ought to do. Brother, I must once more acquaint you with my chief design in making this visit to confer about religious matters, and that our young men agree with me in this, and want to love God and leave off their former bad courses.

"Brother, with regard to what I have mentioned about religious matters, it may be some people may not think as I do, or may think slightly of these matters; but I am fixed in my principles and shall always abide by them.

"I am glad I have an opportunity of mentioning these several matters in presence of such a large audience of young and old people. The great God observes all that passes in our hearts and hears all that we say to one another." He then finished with a solemn act of prayer and thanksgiving, which he performed very devoutly.

The next day the governor returned them a kind and suitable answer, promising that care should be taken to persevere in their religious progress and wished them a prosperous journey.

It appears that there has been an immediate awakening amongst some of these Indians, more especially of late, when Papoonahoal, who is now their chief, apprehends himself called to preach to them, in which service he was, some time after, joined by two or three more. They appear very earnest in promoting true piety which they apprehended is an inward work, by which the heart is changed from bad to good which they express by the heart becoming soft, and being filled with good. In this disposition they absolutely refused to join the other Indians in the prosecution of the war; letting them know they would not join them in it though they should be killed or made slaves or (as they express it) Negroes of them. And I understood that their chief declared that whatever argument might be used in defense of war he was fully persuaded that when God made men he never intended they should kill or destroy one another.—Friends had several solid opportunities with them. They regularly attended our meetings during their stay in town, kept themselves quite free from drink and behaved soberly and orderly, after expressing their satisfaction with what they had heard from Friends, which they said exactly answered to their own religious prospect. They returned home and were accompanied as far as Bethlehem by a Friend who made some further observation upon their conversation and conduct on the way, and is as follows:

The behaviour of these Indians in general was commendable, but particularly the behaviour of Papoonahoal, their chief which afforded me some satisfaction as well as a great deal of instruction; for his deportment was such as manifested his mind to be quiet and easy, accompanied with a becoming solidity and gravity. He dropped several expressions which, as they were interpreted to me, appeared to be worthy of note. Being asked what he thought of war, he answered, "It has been told to my heart that man was not made for that end, therefore I have ceased from war; yet I have not laboured to bring about a peace so much as I ought to have done. I was made weak for that end by the bad spirit's reviving to overcome the good in my heart, but I hope the good spirit will overcome the bad, and then I shall labour heartily to bring about a peace. I have often thought it strange that the Christians are such great warriors, and I have wondered they are not greater lovers of peace, for" said he, "from the time God first showed himself to my mind, and put his goodness in my heart, I found myself in such a temper that I thought if the flesh had been whipped off me with horsewhips I could have borne it without being angry at those that did it."

As we were riding on the way I had a mind to say something to him concerning our Saviour's words and good examples when on earth. I desired the interpreter to ask him if he was disposed to hear these things. He answered, "Such words are very good and would be very acceptable at a fit time. Such things are awful, and should be spoke of at a solemn time, for the heart is soft, and they will go into it and not be lost; but when the heart is hard they will not go into it, but fall off from the heart and so are lost, and such words should not be lost, but at a fit time I would be glad to hear of these things."

Concerning people reasoning about religion, he said: "When people speak of these things they are apt to stand in opposition one against the other, as they strove to throw each other down, or to see which is the wisest. Now these things should not be; but whilst one is speaking the other should hold his head down until the first has done, and then speak without being in heat or angry."

I asked him what he thought was the cause of the alterations of the times, and why they were so changed from what they had been some years past. He answered, "People are grown cross to each other. If they live in love it would not be so; but they grow proud and covetous, which causes God to be angry and to send dry and hot summers and hard winters, and also sickness amongst the people, which he would not do if they loved one another and would do as he would have them."

Being at the Indian town near Bethlehem and setting in company with two or three persons which were conversing on religious matters, he said, "I am apprehensive that I have a feeling and sense in my own heart, whereby I know when people speak from the head, or when they speak from the heart."

I told him many of my Friends as well as myself had been thoughtful about the Indians last winter, and had desires for their welfare, and that my heart was made to love many of them though I had never seen them. He replied, "I believe this love was of God, for though you did not know we should come down, nor ourselves did we know it, yet God did. Therefore he inclined your heart towards us that you might be the more glad and make us the more welcome when we did come."

I understood by the interpreter that this Indian no sooner felt the power of God on his heart to his comfort, but he endeavoured to make the other Indians sensible of the same, and laboured to turn their minds to a search after what he had himself so happily found. One of those Indians who after some time joined him in this work was at first approved by Papoonahoal, but showing an inclination to fall back to some of his corrupt ways, Papoonahoal desired him to be silent, for, says he, "you will spoil the people by speaking from a bad heart. Go get your own heart made clean first and then come and speak to the people."

The Interpreter gave me an account of the manner in which Papoonahoal was first enlightened, which was as follows: "He was formerly a drunken man, but the death of his father bringing sorrow over his mind, he fell into a thoughtful melancholy state, in which state his eyes were turned to behold the earth and to consider things that are thereon, and seeing the folly and wickedness that prevailed, his sorrows increased, and it was given to him to believe that there was a great power that had created all these things; and his mind was turned from beholding this lower world to look towards him that had created it, and strong desires were begot in his heart for a further knowledge of his Creator; nevertheless the Almighty was not yet pleased to be found of him; but his desire increasing, he forsook his friends and went into the woods in great bitterness of spirit. The other Indians missing him and fearing evil had befallen him, went from the town in search of him but could not find him, but at the end of five days it pleased God to appear to him to his comfort, and to give him a sight not only of his own inward state, but also an acquaintance into the works of nature. He also apprehended a sense was given him of the virtues and nature of several herbs, roots, plants and trees, and the different relations they had one to another, and he was made sensible that man stood in the nearest relation to God of any other part of the Creation. It was at this time he was made sensible of his duty to God, and he came home rejoicing and endeavoured to put into practice what he had apprehended was required of him."

The morning I parted with them at Bethlehem I told him I intended to set my face homeward, and if any of you have a word of advice to give me, I shall hear it gladly. After some pause Papoonahoal spoke as follows:

"Brother, it discovers a good disposition in you to love to hear good counsel. There are some people that set light by what I say, and will not hear me. Since I at first had desires after God, people of different notions about religion have spoke to me, all directing me to their particular way, but there is but one way to the place of happiness which God has prepared for his creature man. Brother, there are none that ever spoke such good words to me as I have heard from the Quakers; for what they say answers exactly to what has been told my heart before I saw them. When I left home I resolved not to speak to the Quakers but to harken and hear what they would speak to me. I have heard a voice speak to my heart and say the Quakers are right. It may be a wrong voice, but I believe it is the true voice. However if the goodness which I feel in my heart remain with me, I shall come again to see the Quakers, and if I continue to grow strong, I hope the time will come that I shall be joined in close fellowship with them."

Since the foregoing account, Papoonahoal, the Indian Chief, in conversation said that he thought the Quakers walked the nearest to what Jesus Christ had required us to do, and that he thought war was unlawful. When some in company argued for a defensive war, and asserted that if a man was to come and kill any of them when it was in their power to prevent it, they should be accountable for their own death, the old man answered that he understood the white people had a book which God had ordered to be wrote for them, wherein they were informed that God had made the world; and that he had sent his son, Jesus Christ, into the world to show us how we should live. To this it was replied that this was true. "Well then," said Papoonahoal, "why did not Jesus Christ fight when the people took him to kill him?" He also added that he believed the white people were very wicked as they had so great an advantage of that book and lived so contrary to it.

As Others Saw Woolman
(Letters from the Journey to England)

Letters 1–3 are from Samuel Emlen to his wife.[46]

1.

Seventh day Morning. 5 mo 2, 1772 On board the Mary & Elizabeth off Newcastle

I wish to make thee, my dearest, as little solicitous about me as I may by frequent communication to thee, and am now set down to tell thee, I was favored with a good night's rest. I went to bed early, and we are in much harmony among ourselves, mutual kindness prevails, and I am hopeful that we in the cabin especially shall continue in these dispositions during our confinement together. John Woolman is as free and open as I at any time remember him; he has been several times in my stateroom, and inclines to make it a receptacle for some of his matters which are not proper to be in the steerage loose.

---

46. The letters in this section are drawn from two sources, Henry Cadbury's "Sailing to England with Woolman" and Cadbury's *John Woolman in England*. The first selections consist of passages from letters by fellow passenger Samuel Emlen, a minister in Philadelphia Yearly Meeting and a close companion to Woolman on the voyage. Cadbury quotes from a letter written in Philadelphia by Joseph Oxley of Norwich who was concluding his own long period of ministry in America: "Samuel Emlen, at our last monthly meeting at Philadelphia, laid before the meeting a concern he had on his mind to pay a religious visit to Friends in some parts of Great Britain; also another Friend, John Woolman, a wise and sensible man having a good gift in the ministry and well approved of, has a concern of like kind more particularly to Yorkshire." Cadbury, *John Woolman in England*, 29.

Margaret Haines I suppose was kindly careful for him and he is much better provided with necessaries than thou may perhaps expect.

I think of thee often with fervent love, and my prayer is that the God of all true blessing may be thy shield, helper, counselor and everlasting salvation. I humblingly comfortingly feel him near, and am allowed prostrately to worship in present renewed confirmation that He the Lord is good. He is and hath to the properly dependent been a stronghold to them in the day of need or trouble, and that he knoweth them who trust in him. My dear love to our children, our honored father, brother Wilson and sisters and to our Friends and companions in the Truth. I salute thee with a kindness of heart that I cannot fully utter, and hope to ever be in truest affection.

Thine faithfully,
Sam'l Emlen Junr.

2.

Ship Mary & Elizabeth, First day morning, 5 mo. 3. 1772

... As opportunities to England from New York are frequent, desire brother and sisters there to write me often. I shall be glad to hear of their welfare and thro' their pens often of thee and our near connections in Philadelphia.

John Woolman just now tells me he is pretty well, his mind feels easy and that he is quite contented with his lodging. He was just now in my stateroom in which most of his clothes and sea store are. It is a receptacle for them and I think far more proper than the steerage, he having access thither frequent or when he inclines. He is more free and conversable than some expected and expressed himself glad in having me so near him.

3.

London, seventh day, 6th of 6 month 1772

... Our Friend Woolman came frequently into the Cabin and gang-way at bottom of cabin stairs, where was a box or case on which he used to sit and spend much time either reading or sewing. He kept I think much within his usual restrictions on board, tho not so confined as to be unwilling to partake of some part of our stores. We had meetings publicly every first day except the 3d of last month, the day of our leaving the land or capes, in which I trust the testimony of Truth was at least preserved from suffering. The captain chose to encourage such opportunities and came more than once on weekdays to our more select religious sittings. I think highly of him as a ship master, a good seaman, judicious on deck and courteous in the cabin.

My kind love to our cousin Elizabeth Hatkinson. Her son John I think is fatter than when we embarked. My acquaintance with him increased my esteem for him. I invited him to be with me at J. Eliot's, but he is not come to town, not inclining to leave John Woolman and J. Tilladams in the ship when Cousin Logan and I did, in the English Channel of Dungeness about 15 miles from Dover....

4.

Except for this first letter written by John Pemberton in America to Joseph Row in London, the remaining letters are by English Friends.

Philadelphia 4 mo. 28, 1772

This goes per Capt. Sparks with whom our dear Friends John Woolman and Samuel Emlen embarks, Thou knows the latter who is grown a sound good minister and I hope will have acceptable service. The first is a truly upright man but walks in a straiter path than some good folk are led, or do travel in. He is a good minister, a sensible man, and though he may appear singular, yet from a close knowledge of him he will be found to be a man of a sweet clean spirit and preserved from harsh censure of those who do not see and conform as he does. It will be safest for Friends with you to leave him much to his own feelings, and to walk and steer in that path which proves most easy to him, without using much arguments or persuasion. He will do nothing knowingly against the Truth, and has had long experience in the Truth. He is much beloved and respected among us, and I doubt not will on close acquaintance be so to the truly religious with you.

I have recommended him to thy house or John Townsend's. You live as I apprehend in the simplicity and plainness that will prove most easy to him, though I know there are other good Friends whose hearts and houses have been, and I doubt not still are, open to such messengers, and who hospitably entertain strangers. If it does not suit thy family tell my friend John

Townsend what I have done and settle the matter between you. I expect he may remain on board the vessel until she gets to London. However I hope thou'll learn in season to meet him. Little will content him, and the poorer the fare the more acceptable.

5.

From an English Friend, William Forster, to his cousin Rebecca Haydock in America dated 8 mo 16, 1772.

The remarkable appearance of your countryman John Woolman who is now with Sarah Morris and her niece in Yorkshire attracts the notice of many. His steady uniform deportment, his meekness and unaffected humility, his solidity, no less in conversation than in his ministry, which is instructing and edifying, creates much esteem and well corresponds with his appearance. I think your ministers in general far exceed ours though we are favoured with several eminent ones, among whom is a Friend now at our house of whom I suppose thou hast heard, Sophia Hume, a native of South Carolina, as plain in her dress for a woman as J. Woolman for a man...

6.

From a letter to Sally Tuke, dated 8 mo 9th 1772. The writer incorrectly calls him John Woolmer.

My dear Sally:

...Our very valuable Friends John Woolmer and Sarah Morris were at this meeting yesterday was a week, which was exceedingly crowded, part through curiosity to see John's particular dress, and part I hope for a better motive, whom I apprehend when away well satisfied with what they heard from the man whose uncouth appearance will be likely to prejudice many. But he is certainly a very deep minister that searches things quite to the bottom, greatly exercised in a life of self-denial and humility. Therefore must the will of the creature be more subdued and the better fitted to receive the mystery of the kingdom, which I believe through much obedience are largely opened. And I can't but think Providence hath some wise end in what seems difficult to reconcile with man's wisdom. Perhaps it may be intended to wean many from the things which outwardly adorn the body, and likewise other luxuries and delicacys [sic], too much prevailing amongst those in exalted stations as to this world's enjoyments, besides the testimony he finds it a duty to bear against the iniquitous trading in Negroes that so deeply affected his mind as to make his tears both as meat and drink for many days... .

I was favored to be present at an opportunity at W. Fairbank's where he opened his reasons for several things and gave...advice to the youth of whom there was several present. May it be properly impressed upon each mind.

7.

The following excerpts describe in detail how Woolman looked. The first is from Mary Andrew's Book Of Extracts, *dated 1812. The passage, however, is dated 8 mo. 2nd 1772.*

John Woolman, a publick Friend from America, was at Sheffield on a religious visit. He was remarkable for the singularity of his dress. His shoes were of uncured leather, tied with leather strings, his stockings of white yarn, his coat, waistcoat, and breeches of a strong kind of cloth undyed, the natural colour of the wool, the buttons of wood with brass shanks; his shirt of cotton unbleached, about 14d. pr yard, fastened at the neck with three large buttons of the same stuff, without either cravat or handkerchief about his neck; his hat a very good one was white, his countenance grave, sensible and expressive; in conversation rather reserved (except with a few individuals) being at all times more ready to hear than to offer the sacrifice of fools. Though many might think him whimsical from the odd appearance he made—he was a man of great understanding, and had very good natural abilities; of a mild and benevolent disposition, as might be easily discovered by the natural unaffected simplicity of his manners, which never failed of producing respect from all who were acquainted with him.

He said the cause why he appeared so was that he believed it to be his duty to bear a testimony not in words only, but to be a sign to the people, to testify against the pride and extravagancy of those days, which greatly abounded with superfluities.

He avoided the company of the rich and great, and would visit the habitations of the poor (who were well esteemed) with pleasure; he loved to see the honest simplicity of those who lived in remote parts of the world, and who were not over-anxious about riches, etc. His diet was plain, chiefly consisting of bread, milk or butter, and he was truly a valuable, good man, a friend and well wisher to mankind universally, of whom it might be said, "an Israelite indeed, in whom there was no guile." He was taken ill of the small pox at York 9th mo. 27th 1772, and departed this life in full assurance of eternal happiness.

8.

Woolman attended High Flatts Monthly Meeting on August 5, 1772. An unknown Friend made the following note of his appearance.

John Woolman appears to me to be a man of very deep experience in the things of God, and coming up in obedience to the Light of Christ was led out of all superfluity in meat, drink and apparel, being a pattern of remarkable plainness, humility and self denial. His dress as follows: a white hat; a coarse raw linen shirt, without anything about the neck; his coat, waistcoat and breeches of white coarse woolen cloth with wool buttons on; his coat without cuffs; white yarn stockings and shoes of uncured leather with bands instead of buckles, so that he was all white.[47]

---

47. This description agrees with the preceding, except that his shirt in this account is linen, which is more probable since cotton would be likely to involve slave labor.

Study Guide

These topics and questions are in two parts. General Topics and Questions are intended to help readers focus attention on particular themes, collect examples, and draw conclusions. The second part, Topics and Questions on the Text, follows the order of the Source Book and raises questions which relate to specific chapters or passages, and at times directs the reader to related passages in other parts of the Source Book.

General Topics and Questions

1. Social change agents generally need certain conditions in order to carry on their work. To what extent are these conditions present in Woolman's situation?

   a. a supportive philosophy of religion
   b. a community to which they belong
   c. a way of making a living
   d. some means of communicating with like-minded people and with a larger public
   e. an ethos which is at least tolerant of what they are trying to do

2. Social change agents use a variety of means. Which of these means does Woolman use? Which ones does he emphasize?

   a. helping people directly with food, clothing, and shelter
   b. acting as an advocate for the oppressed
   c. empowering the oppressed
   d. making peace by mediating or reducing tension
   e. making a witness by changing their own life-styles

3. Woolman was far ahead of his time in his concern for animals and for the environment. In which passages does he express these concerns? What does he see? What does he think should be done? What does he do himself?

4. Woolman's concern about slavery broadened to include other forms of oppression. What other groups or individuals does Woolman become concerned about? What actions does he take? Does he seem to be less concerned about other groups? If yes, how do you explain this?

5. Woolman was concerned with the spiritual condition of both the oppressed and their oppressors. What do you think of his approach as a way of dealing with oppressors? Imagine yourself as trying to use this approach by writing a letter to someone in authority.

6. In his *Journal*, in the essay "On Schools," and in *A First Book for Children*, Woolman shows great interest in the education and development of children and young people. What does he do or advocate doing? To what extent are his ideas applicable today?

7. In his writings Woolman often deals with economic matters—rents, interest rates, trade, employment, prices, inheritance—and the motives that drive economic decisions. What specifically does he see, and what suggestions does he make? Are his ideas on economics applicable today?

8. To what extent does Woolman draw on the Bible for inspiration and guidance? To what extent does he use Scripture passages to support his actions? How does his use of Scripture compare with his reliance on inward guidance or on prayer? Which passages illustrate what you see?

9. Woolman talks about "leadings" and "movings" of the spirit. What is Woolman's process for finding divine guidance? How is your own process of finding inward guidance similar to or different from Woolman's?

Topics and Questions on the Text

The Journal chapter 1

10. In chapter 1, Woolman writes about his first twenty-two years. Compare Woolman's experience with your own in regard to finding direction,

feeling and responding to concerns, and relating to other people. What would you include in a chapter like this about your life? Write your own chapter 1.

11. What do you make of Woolman's childhood dream? Why do you think he included it? What memorable dream(s) would you include from your childhood?

12. After the incident with the robins, what conclusion does Woolman reach about the nature of human beings? Does his response to the incident surprise you? How do you interpret his response?

13. On two occasions Woolman is moved to speak in Meeting. How does he determine whether and how he should speak? How do you interpret these two experiences of speaking?

14. When Woolman is first asked to write an instrument of slavery, how does he respond? How does he respond the second time? What do you think he is learning about slavery? About what he might do?

The Journal chapter 2

15. Why would there be a difference between the spiritual condition of people in the old settlements vs. those in the new settlements?

16. Does Woolman appear to be concerned mostly with slaves? Or with slave owners? Or with both? What is the "dark gloominess" that he sees?

The Journal chapter 3

17. Woolman continues to be asked to write instruments of slavery. How do these responses compare with earlier ones?

18. What does Woolman mean when he speaks of trying to rid himself of "outward cumbers"? Do you think one has to do this in order to be

an effective agent of social change, or is it better to make oneself more secure first?

The Journal chapter 4

19. Woolman tries to make it clear that the experience he describes in the first paragraph was not a dream. What was it then, and how does it differ from the dream in chapter 1? Have you ever had an experience of this kind?

20. Do you think that Woolman's practice of giving money to slaves, or to their masters to pass on to their slaves, is an effective way of challenging the system of slavery?

The Journal chapter 5

21. How does working on the slavery issue through an organization such as the Yearly Meeting differ from the more personal efforts Woolman tried earlier?

22. To what extent does Woolman seem to be effective in the Yearly Meeting itself, and perhaps as a result of that Meeting's decisions? Given what he tells us, how do you interpret his involvement and his way of reporting what happened?

The Journal chapter 7

23. What do you see as Woolman's purpose in visiting the Yearly Meeting in Newport?

24. How do you feel about Woolman's leaving his family for four months in order to carry out this purpose? What is revealed about his relations with his family in Letters 1 through 5 (see Selected Letters)?

25. Mercy Redman was travelling in the ministry at the same time, visiting some of the same places. Compare Woolman's account of the journey with Mercy Redman's account. What does her journal reveal about his journal?

26. Woolman has a strong inclination to "petition the Legislature" concerning the slave trade. Why do you think he does not go through with it? Do you think he might be more likely to petition the government if he were in our situation today?

27. What do you think of Woolman's observations on the economic and environmental problems he saw on the island of Nantucket? Do you see parallels between what he saw and our situation today?

The Journal chapter 8

28. What do you see as Woolman's purpose in making a difficult and dangerous journey to visit the American Indians at Wyalusing? If he was not trying to convert them to Christianity, then what was he doing?

29. Read "The Substance of Some Conversation with Paponahoal" (in Other Writings by Woolman) and "Some Account of the Behaviour and Sentiments of a Number of Well Disposed Indians" (in the Related Writings by Contemporaries). What do these writings suggest about Woolman's purposes in traveling to visit the Indians? What do they tell us about the Delawares themselves? Geoffrey Plank observes that the Quakers were eager "to project their own beliefs" onto their accounts about the Indians (158). How do you see this as a complication in reading these accounts?

30. On the journey, Woolman encounters a Moravian missionary, David Zeisberger, though Woolman does not give his name. Zeisberger had learned Delaware and was intent on converting the Indians. Woolman does not know Delaware, and has not brought an interpreter. How does

Woolman communicate? What impression do you think he made? How successful was the visit?

31. What do you think of Woolman's observations and reflections during this journey? Does he seem to view of the Indians sentimentally or realistically?

32. What in Woolman's experience might be applied today to understanding the conflicts between cultures and ethnic groups?

The Journal chapter 10

33. The illness reported in chapter 10 is the one referred to in chapter 12 during which Woolman had a remarkable vision. What is your reaction to Woolman's attitude toward death and dying?

34. What do you think Woolman is trying to convey in his two dictated statements?

The Journal chapter 12

35. What do you see as Woolman's purpose in going to England? What do you think he achieved? (See his essay "Concerning the Ministry," letters 13–17, and As Others Saw Woolman in Related Writings)

36. What does Woolman particularly notice in his observations about what is happening in England? What is revealed about conditions in England? What do these passages reveal about Woolman?

37. Woolman has been making self-denying resolutions for years. What new resolutions does he make in England? How do they strike you?

38. Compare Woolman's vision in this chapter with the one at the beginning of chapter 4. What do you make of this second experience? What does it seem to mean to Woolman?

39. Many people have read Woolman's "vision" in *The Journal* chapter 12 as a significant event in his life. He had the vision in 1770, two and a half years before writing this description. Are the effects of the "vision" evident in comparisons of his writings from before 1770 and after? It might be helpful to compare *Journal* chapter 12 (and possibly chapter 11, not included in the *Source Book*) with earlier chapters, and to compare "Remarks on Sundry Subjects," and "Concerning the Ministry" with earlier essays. Are his interests and concerns changing or shifting? Does he rely upon the Bible differently? Is there any change in his writing style? Questions of this kind are difficult but may reveal important aspects of his ideas and his ways of expressing them.

Selected Letters

40. Personal letters often give a different impression of the writer than do journals, essays, and other more formal writings. What impressions would you have of Woolman if you had read only these letters?

41. Reading the letters addressed to Sarah Woolman (#1, 2, 5, 7, 9, 14, 15) and to other members of his family (#4, 13, 16, 17), what is your impression of Woolman's relationship with his family? Letter #15 seems especially revealing. How do you interpret that letter?

42. How are Woolman's concerns and inner leadings, as expressed in the letters, different from what he says about these matters in *The Journal*?

43. Letter #11 seems to be a follow-up to a conversation. What is the central idea of the letter? How do this central idea and the six paragraphs relate to ideas in *The Journal* and the essays?

44. Letter #12 has no name attached, but it appears to be a follow-up to a meeting of ministers and elders. What are Woolman's concerns in this letter? How do they relate to ideas in *The Journal*?

45. Letter #16 is addressed to the children of Stephen Comfort (in other words to Woolman's son-in-law and his siblings). What seems to be his purpose in writing this letter?

46. What is Woolman's state of mind in Letter #17, which may have been the last letter he wrote? What does his final sentence suggest about his expectations for returning home?

Selections from Woolman's Essays

"A Plea for the Poor"

47. Note Woolman's idea that there is "one common interest from which our own is inseparable" which is "to turn all the treasures that we possess into the channel of universal love." Is this a workable goal or is it too idealistic?

48. What is the central statement that Woolman is making in chapter 5? How effective do you think it might have been for readers in his day? How effective would it be today?

"Serious Considerations On Trade"

49. What do you think of Woolman's ideas on trade? What relevance might they have for us in our global economy?

"Serious Considerations on Various Subjects of Importance"

50. What does Woolman see as the objectives of education? How do you interpret his ideas about class size, teacher qualifications, and the use of external motivations, such as grades?

51. After reading Woolman's *A First Book for Children*, how useful do you think this book would be in teaching children to read?

"Remarks on Sundry Subjects"

52. In this last collection of essays, what do you think Woolman has learned about slavery? About the need for education? About the condition of the poor?

53. In the last three paragraphs, Woolman offers a vision of what the world might be like if people followed the "leadings of the Holy Spirit." To what extent does this vision have appeal today?

54. In "Remarks on Sundry Subjects," Woolman deals with ideas about simple living, stewardship, moderate employment, and attention to the needs of all. How relevant are his ideas today?

"Concerning the Ministry"

55. Does Woolman have any definite purpose or plan as he travels across England? What does he say is guiding him? What new insights about ministry seem to have come to him? What new problems does he seem to have encountered in England?

56. Several passages in "Concerning the Ministry" seem to have large implications about how a person can find effective words to speak (or write), how one finds direction, or how one gets through a difficult situation. How do you interpret these passages?

Other Writings by Woolman

Conversations on the True Harmony of Mankind

57. The *Conversations* is Woolman's only known written dialogue. Why do you think he chose this form?

58. If the Laborer in these dialogues speaks Woolman's mind, what can we learn about Woolman's approach to people who may be oppressors but are ignorant of what they are doing?

59. In his other writings we have seen Woolman's awareness of the connection of things. What specific connections does he call attention to in these conversations?

60. Woolman makes no mention of slavery in the *Conversations*. Why do you think this is?

61. The Laborer offers some specific suggestions on improving the condition of the poor. What are they? Do they strike you as being practical?

62. Woolman was not an expert in writing dialogue, but *Conversations* can be read as a kind of one-act play. Rewrite it for the purpose of starting a group discussion.

63. Write a dialogue of your own that addresses a contemporary situation, with characters appropriate to that situation.

"The Substance of Some Conversation with Paponahoal the Indian Chief..."

64. Compare this brief account with the longer account in Related Writings by Contemporaries and in chapter 8 of *The Journal*. Where do they agree? Where do they differ?

65. What impression do you get of Sarah Woolman from her words at the bottom of "The Substance..."?

A First Book for Children

66. What are Woolman's objectives in this little book for children? What does Woolman want children to know and be able to do at the end

of their course of study using this book? He seems to have objectives beyond their learning to read. How effective would this book be in helping them achieve these other objectives?

67. How do you picture this book being used in an elementary classroom?

68. Try to locate a copy of the *New England Primer*, which was in use at the same time as Woolman's, and was still in use in the 19th century. It went through many editions. The shorter Westminster Catechism made up more than half the book. *The Primer* usually included the Lord's Prayer, the Creed, and the Ten Commandments, along with some somber verses that may, among other things, have been included to keep children aware of their own mortality. Some editions included a woodcut of a Protestant martyr being burned at the stake in Queen Mary's time, while his wife and ten children watch. By comparison, what does Woolman's *A First Book for Children* reveal about his attitude toward humanity?

Related Writings by Contemporaries

69. Reading the excerpts from Redman's "Journal," were her purposes different from Woolman's? What does she report that he does not and vice versa?

70. Redman's account of visiting Quaker meetings has a different quality from Woolman's. What do you observe about her descriptions and his descriptions? How does her writing change your ideas about what Woolman was doing on his journeys?

71. Regarding "Some Account of...a Number of Well Disposed Indians," do you agree with Geoffrey Plank that the Quakers are projecting their own beliefs onto the Indians in this account (see Question 29 above)?

72. What do the letters by other people confirm or change in your ideas about Woolman? Do the letters by other people offer additional insights?

Resources

Barbour, Hugh, and J. William Frost. *The Quakers*. New York: Greenwood, 1988.

Birkel, Michael. *A Near Sympathy: The Timeless Quaker Wisdom of John Woolman*. Richmond, IN: Friends United Press, 2003.

"British Settlements: Middle Colonies." *Encyclopedia of North American Colonies*. 1993 ed.

Brock, Peter. *The Quaker Peace Testimony, 1660 to 1914*. York, England: Sessions Book Trust, 1990.

Brinton, Howard H. *Friends for 350 Years: The History and Beliefs of the Society of Friends Since George Fox Started the Quaker Movement*. Wallingford, PA: Pendle Hill, 2002.

Cadbury, Henry J. *John Woolman in England 1772: A Documentary Supplement*. Philadelphia: Friends Historical Society, 1971.

———. "Sailing to England with John Woolman." *Quaker History* 55 (1966): 88–103.

Cady, Edwin H. *John Woolman*. New York: Washington Square, 1966.

Carey, Brycchan, *From Peace to Freedom: Quaker Rhetoric and the Birth of American Antislavery, 1657-1761*. New Haven: Yale University Press, 2012.

Carroll, Kenneth. "A Look at the Quaker Revival of 1756." *Quaker History* 65 (1976): 63–80.

Christian, William A. "Inwardness and Outward Concerns: A Study of John Woolman's Thought." *Quaker History* 67 (1978): 88–104.

Couser, G. Thomas. *American Autobiography*. Amherst: University of Massachusetts Press, 1979.

Drake, Thomas E. *Quakers and Slavery*. New Haven: Yale University Press, 1950.

Fox, George. *The Journal of George Fox*. ed. John L. Nickalls. London: London Yearly Meeting, 1952.

Heller, Mike. *The Tendering Presence: Essays on John Woolman*. Wallingford, PA: Pendle Hill Publications, 2003.

James, Sydney V. *A People Among Peoples: Quaker Benevolence in Eighteenth-Century America*. Cambridge: Harvard University Press, 1963.

Jones, Rufus M. "Evidence of the Influence of Quietism on John Woolman." *Friends Intelligencer* 105 (Third Month 6, 1948): 131–32.

Marietta, Jack D. *The Reformation of American Quakerism, 1748–1783*. Philadelphia: University of Pennsylvania Press, 1984.

Moulton, Phillips P. "The Influence of the Writings of John Woolman." *Quaker History* 60 (1971), 3–13.

———. "John Woolman: Exemplar of Ethics." *Quaker History* 54 (1965), 81–93.

———. "John Woolman's Approach to Social Action as Exemplified in Relation to Slavery." *Church History* 35 (1966): 399–410.

Nash, Gary B., and Jean R. Soderlund. *Freedom by Degrees: Emancipation in Pennsylvania and Its Aftermath*. New York: Oxford University Press, 1991.

Olmsted, Sterling. *Motions of Love: Woolman as Mystic and Activist*. Wallingford, PA: Pendle Hill, 1993.

———. "Woolman and Gandhi and Human Betterment: or The Yoga of Peacemaking." *Proceedings: Conference on Quaker Studies on Human Betterment*. Swarthmore, PA: Friends Association for Higher Education, 1988. 43–50.

Pickett, Ralph H. "A Religious Encounter: John Woolman and David Zeisberger." *Quaker History* 79 (Fall 1990): 77–92.

Plank, Geoffrey. *John Woolman's Path to the Peaceable Kingdom: A Quaker in the British Empire*. Philadelphia: University of Pennsylvania Press, 2012.

Proud, James. *John Woolman and the Affairs of Truth*. San Francisco: Inner Light Books, 2011.

Reynolds, Reginald. *The Wisdom of John Woolman*. 1948. London: Friends Home Service Committee, 1972.

Rosenblatt, Paul. *John Woolman*. New York: Twayne, 1969.

Shea, Daniel B. *Spiritual Autobiography in Early America*. Princeton: Princeton University Press, 1968.

Shi, David E. *The Simple Life: Plain Living and High Thinking in American Culture*. New York: Oxford University Press, 1985.

Slaughter, Thomas. *The Beautiful Soul of John Woolman, Apostle of Abolition*. New York: Hill and Wang, 2009.

Soderlund, Jean R. *Quakers & Slavery: A Divided Spirit*. Princeton: Princeton University Press, 1985.

Stewart, Margaret E. "John Woolman's 'Kindness beyond Expression': Collective Identity vs. Individualism and White Supremacy." *Early American Literature* 26.3 (1991): 251–275.

Terrell, Thomas E., Jr. "John Woolman: The Theology of a Public Order." *Quaker History* 71 (1982): 16–30.

Tolles, Frederick B. *Meeting House and Counting House: The Quaker Merchants of Colonial Philadelphia 1682–1763*. 1948. New York: Norton, 1963.

———. "Of the Best Sort but Plain': The Quaker Esthetic." *American Quarterly* 11.4 (1959): 484–502.

United States Dept. of Commerce. Bureau of the Census. *Historical Statistics of the United States, Colonial times to 1970*. Washington: GPO, 1975.

Woolman, John. *A First Book for Children: A, B, C, D, etc.* 3rd ed. London: Phillips, n.d.

———. *Conversations on the True Harmony of Mankind And How It May Be Promoted*. ed. Sterling Olmsted. Philadelphia: Wider Quaker Fellowship, Friends World Committee for Consultation, Section of the Americas, 1987.

———. *The Journal and Essays of John Woolman*. ed. Amelia Mott Gummere. New York: Macmillan, 1922.

———. *The Journal and Major Essays of John Woolman*. ed. Phillips P. Moulton. 1971. Richmond, IN: Friends United Press, 1989.

Sources of the Text

Selections from *The Journal*:

All are from Phillips Moulton's edition, *The Journal and Major Essays of John Woolman* (see Selected Bibliography).

Selected Letters:

Letters 1–5, 7–1, and 12–16 are from Gummere's edition, *The Journal and Essays of John Woolman* (see Selected Bibliography).

Letters 6 and 11 are from *Friends Miscellany* (Philadelphia: John and Isaac Comly, 1831) Vol. 1.

Selections from Woolman's Essays:

Selections of "A Plea for the Poor" are from Moulton's edition, *The Journal and Major Essays of John Woolman*.

"Serious Considerations on Trade" is from Gummere's edition, *The Journal and Essays of John Woolman*. "Serious Considerations on Various Subjects of Importance (On Schools)," also found in Gummere.

Selections of "Remarks on Sundry Subjects" are from a microfiche copy of a printing by Mary Hinde, London, 1773.

"Concerning the Ministry" is from Gummere's edition, *The Journal and Essays of John Woolman*. Two passages were corrected, based upon LS TEMP MSS 1002, Library of the Society of Friends (LSF), London.

Other Writings by Woolman:

Selections from *Conversations on the True Harmony of Mankind and How it May Be Promoted* are from Sterling Olmsted, ed., Philadelphia: Wider

Quaker Fellowship, Friends World Committee for Consultation, Section of the Americas, 1987.

"The Substance of Some Conversations with Paponahoal the Indian Chief" is from Vol. 13, p. 23, manuscript, Pemberton Papers, Historical Society of Pennsylvania.

Images of *A First Book for Children*, 3rd edition (Philadelphia: Crukshank, n.d.) are from the one surviving original located in the Library of the Society of Friends (LSF), London.

Related writings by Contemporaries:

Mercy Redman's "Journal" is from a manuscript at Friends Historical Library, Swarthmore College.

"Some Accounts of the Behavior and Sentiments of a Number of Well-Disposed Indians" is from a manuscript at Friends Historical Library, Swarthmore College.

As Others Saw Woolman, letters 1–3 are from Cadbury's "Sailing to England with John Woolman." Selections 4–8 are found in Cadbury's *John Woolman in England: A Documentary Supplement* (see Selected Bibliography).

CPSIA information can be obtained at www.ICGtesting.com
Printed in the USA
BVOW010004120613

323048BV00005B/36/P